FEEDING YOUR DOG AND CAT

THE TRUTH!

Dr. Jarvis Williams, DVM

The contents of this work, including, but not limited to, the accuracy of events, people, and places depicted; opinions expressed; permission to use previously published materials included; and any advice given or ations advocated are solely the responsibility of the author, who assumes all liability for said work and indemnifies the publisher against any claims stemming from publication of the work.

Hardcover ISBN: 978-1-7379167-1-0
Paperback ISBN: 978-1-7379167-0-3

Visit www.jarviswrites.page for dozens of dog and cat informative blogs, pictures, recipes, and pictures of how to use a turkey roaster to make a lot of dog and cat food easily, cheaply, and fast.

The website also has links to other books by the same author.

The website also has links to other animal and veterinary-oriented authors.

Sign up with your email to receive offers, updates, freebees, and for sneak peeks of new books before anyone else can read them.

DEDICATION

This book is dedicated to the thousands of beloved pets that SUFFERED AND DIED in 2007 because of INTENTIONALLY ALTERED, CONTAMINATED, POLLLUTED, and UNREGULATED, ingredients from CHINA, sold to hundreds of North American commercial pet food manufacturers.

The Chinese government denied the problem, and refused to allow foreign safety officials to investigate.

It led to the biggest pet food recall in history; over 400 brands were removed from shelves.

This book is written to help put the control of our loyal and devoted pets' food back into the safety of our own kitchens.

Written with love to keep future generations of pets safe and healthy.

Dr. Jarvis E. Williams, DVM

Of course, you can feed your dog people food;
But…
You better not feed people dog food.

You don't have to be a scientist to cook your dog food;
But…
You have to be a scientist to cook for a dog food company.

There is a nutritional component to every disease.

EXCERPTS from the BOOK

- It's not unusual for ingredients to have already been processed with heat, solvents, and chemicals, 4 to 6 times, before a pet food company runs them through multiple processes again.

- There have been over fifty recalls of commercial pet foods over the last two years, because the food caused sickness and even death. (That's just the ones we know.)

- The pet food industry has convinced us that feeding dogs and cats is too difficult for us to manage. Well, it would be if we used what they use.

- People are trying to eat "healthy." They want their pets to eat healthy too.

- Feeding your pets only commercial food is like telling Mom to only feed factory-prepared food. (Don't feed your family home-cooked meatloaf, mashed potatoes and gravy, peas and carrots, and apple pie and ice cream.)

- Pet food manufacturers can say anything they want about their products. It may be made out of crank case oil, shoe leather, charcoal, and crushed limestone, but the label can boast that it is "fully balanced and complete."

- Most toxins found in pet food are not added by the pet food company. They are already in the ingredients they use. If a pet gets sick, the manufacturer always blames the supplier.

- There is no government agency overseeing the pet food industry. Not one.

- There are over 500 nutrients in a whole carrot, only ten of which end up in multiple vitamins.

- "Whole food"—the way it comes off the tree, vine, field, or hoof—is what you should feed your pets.

- Cooking for your pet? It is so simple even a caveman can do it. Wait a minute…cavemen did do it.

- For the stomach, eating dry kibble is like eating a "Cup-of-Soup" without adding the water.

- I can't count how many dog owners say that since they started cooking for their dog, their dog's breath will no longer stop a train, or peel paint.

- The perfect diet for a cat is four parakeets a day.

- There is nothing wrong with feeding a cat baby food. Or a chicken pot pie.

- Cat diet RECIPE-SEVEN: Open a can of chicken, and put it on a plate.

- No other organ in the body can double the body's weight and still keep growing indefinitely, except fat.

- Dogs do not lose weight by exercising; only by reducing caloric intake.

- Many "experts" that provide testimonials about pet diets make up for their ignorance by punctuating their nutty notions with vehement certainty.

- Before the 1940s the annual production of synthetic chemicals was one million tons. Now it is 200 million tons.

- A primary determinant of lifespan is how efficiently one removes toxic byproducts, or the repair of molecular damage caused by these toxins. Nutrition is directly related to both.

- If a roach or mouse was accidently processed in many of the pet foods today, it would actually contribute positively to the quality of the final product.

- Feeding dry kibble is the furthest removed from food in its natural state as possible.

- The terms *organic, human grade, premium, holistic, free-range, high-pro,* and *senior* have no meaning or definition in the pet food industry. Don't believe anything on a bag of pet food.

- Owners say, "I just thought he was getting old." (No, he was suffering from a lifetime of **prison camp food**.)

- Supplement your food with commercial food, rather than supplementing commercial food with your food.

- It's not a surprise that a high percentage of owners already feed significant amounts of leftovers to their pets. When I endorse and encourage feeding "people food" to their pets they seemed relieved. They feel guilty about feeding from the table! Total nonsense.

CONTENTS

INTRODUCTION

As a veterinarian I see nutritional problems in most of my patients.

After upgrading their diet, I always see a change for the good. Owners say, "I just thought he was getting old."

No, he was suffering from **years of prison camp food**; just plain old **malnutrition.**

It doesn't matter what the pets come in for, they get better with higher quality food.

Sure, I treat for disease, do x-rays, and blood work, maybe acupuncture, laser-light treatments, etc. But I ask about their diet too; it is many times part of the problem, and often part of the repair of bad health.

Owners ask what brand of pet food I recommend, or they want assurances that the brand they are feeding is "all right."

My answers have to be:

- I see nutritional problems in your pet.
- You and I get a good meal at least once in a while. Your pet doesn't.
- Kibble (dry pet food) is the farthest thing from what an animal would eat in the wild there is.
- Most pet foods are all the same. None are that great. They are

full of byproducts, renderings, dyes, preservatives, fillers, toxins, genetic modifications, and are processed too many times.

- Soft-moist pet food is even worse than dry kibble.
- Canned is always better because canned food has more meat and fewer carbohydrates than dry kibble; and more water. If it's decent cuts of meat it will cost a lot.
- Consider buying hamburger or chicken, and make your own pet food—it will be cheaper than premium brands—and it's easy. Or at least supplement a diet of kibble with fresh animal protein like eggs, meat, and cheese.
- Look for foods with ingredients you recognize as real food, as it comes from the field, or off the hoof. Not ingredients that you don't recognize.
- Purina now has a canned line called *Beyond,* which uses whole ingredients. Another company, *Freshpet,* offers decent ingredient food in its own refrigerator case in the pet food aisle. There are many other good brands available at pet stores these days. But they are expensive because they use whole foods, not industry leftovers and byproducts.
- Supplement. (See the chapter on supplements.)
- Multivitamins are a joke.
- They can't put enough glucosamine in dog food to make a difference.
- Dogs and cats don't need insoluble fiber. That's like eating toilet paper or sawdust.
- One reason that I can't recommend any brands is because I can't keep track of who owns and manages the brand. Plus, they can change ingredients without changing the label for six months. Good brands are often bought up by large per food companies, but they usually change the formulas and ingredients—and not to make it better. No one can keep up.

- Besides, pet food companies offer a new brand every day... but it's really the same old stuff.
- This is not complicated. You don't have to be a scientist. Make your own pet food from whole ingredients.
- Use variety. A lot of variety.
- Supplement your food with commercial food, rather than supplementing commercial food with your food.

Pet food companies' marketing departments control our choices for feeding our pets with relentless clever, cutesy, warm and fuzzy advertising, and label presentation. They introduce a new variety, or life stage, literally every day...that is supposed to be "new and improved!" Three hundred and fifty new offerings on the shelf every year.

It is all made out of parts of foods and leftovers from the food processing industry: "Franken-food"—scientists trying to make something the same as when it was alive. Nothing can replace whole foods as it comes off the hoof, out of the field, or off the tree or vine. It's like trying to make a watch out of parts from hundreds of different broken ones. It may work...but not well.

We think we are practically killing our dog if we give him a bite of steak.

Even the liner of the bag the food comes in may be toxic.

What happens to it in storage? In a hot boxcar or truck? Or when frozen?

Don't expect to get anything from a pet food label. They are all using the same things.

Nobody is regulating them.

Guess what? You can feed your pet human food.

You don't have to be a scientist to feed your pet any more than you have to be a scientist to cook for your family. Diversity in your diet from the cornucopia of foods available from the average grocery store is healthy for you...and your animals.

There is a nutritional component to every disease in dogs and cats. Improve the diet and the patient will improve no matter what the problem.

If you don't cook for your pet, then buy a commercial food with ingredients you recognize. If you have to look up a mysterious definition, probably don't buy it. Look for "whole foods," not fractions of foods. Change brands regularly. Make extra of your own dinner to share with your pets. (See the chapter on *How to read pet food labels.*)

Of course, you can feed your pet people food. Give them some every day, in fact.

Feed cats ONLY canned food. Dry cat food is a disaster. (See chapter on *Cooking for your cat.*)

Use whole food supplements. Forget multivitamins. (See chapter on *Supplements.*)

Give them some raw meat every once in a while. And liver and kidney. Cheese. Eggs. Carrots.

Don't feed them pig ears, rawhide, and commercially prepared treats. Rawhide type treats have zero nutrition and contain lots of artificial flavor enhancers and preservatives. When swallowed they can swell and cause blockages. They often contain serious contaminants (made in China).

Make your own treats from such things as crackers and cheese, multigrain bread and peanut butter, or vegetables soaked in broth.

FOREWORD

COMMERCIAL PET FOOD CAN BE DEADLY

After 25 years of agreeing with the pet food industry that pet owners should not prepare their pets' food, or grave nutritional deficiencies will result, **I completely changed my mind** since the **Chinese pet food ingredient disaster.**

There have been over 50 pet food recalls in the last two years—just a drop in the bucket in what's still on the shelves and going in your pet.

In 2007 several Chinese companies sold products to pet food ingredient suppliers that claimed to be wheat gluten, corn gluten, and rice protein, but which proved to be wheat flour adulterated with **melamine, cyanuric acid, and other contaminants**. These additives were added **intentionally** to inflate the apparent protein content of the products…passing off inexpensive (and toxic) ingredients for more expensive ones.

Multiple pet food manufacturers bought ingredients from the same source: Menu Foods (who lost 30 million $$ alone in the subsequent recall). The **adulteration** wasn't discovered until reports of **kidney failure and death** in pets were found to be due to the lethal combination of melamine and cyanuric acid. This

mass poisoning caused over **8000 pet deaths** (that we know of). The next year, 300,000 babies in China became ill after drinking baby formula contaminated with melamine and at least six died.

The Chinese government at first **denied** the problem and refused to allow foreign food safety officials to investigate. Ultimately the Chinese government acknowledged the contamination and arrested the managers of two protein byproduct manufacturers. (One committed suicide, others were executed, and some are still in jail.)

These discoveries lead to the **biggest voluntary pet food recall in history** involving over 400 brands. VOLUNTARY! The government didn't call for the recall because there was (and still is) **zero government oversight of the pet food industry**, and no law allowing a governmental recall of pet food even if the FDA, or another agency, wanted to. The pet food companies HAD to do the recall because animals were dying from eating THEIR food.

There have been hundreds of incidents in which pet **treats** made in China have caused dogs and cat to become sick, or die.

It never stops with CHINA! News sources in China recently reported that **pork** from China was **tainted** with the drug *clenbuterol,* a decongestant and bronchodilator and banned in the U.S. by the FDA. Clenbuterol fed to meat production animals can increase the muscle-to-meat ratio, making leaner meat. It is illegally used by athletes and body builders as a performance-enhancer. It has been banned in the U.S. since 1991 and Europe since 1996. Consumers of this contaminated meat suffer from increased heart rate, tremors, headache, nausea, fever, and chills.

The problem list goes on with China: Chinese pork sold as beef after it being soaked in **borax**; rice contaminated with **cadmium**; corn and mushrooms treated with fluorescent bleach; beansprouts with an animal antibiotic residue. There were up to **nine pesticides** found in one sample. One hundred percent of raw Chinese herbal medicines contain **at least one heavy metal,** including cadmium, arsenic, chromium, lead, and mercury.[1]

---

1 Veterinary Practice News, *Chinese Herbs: Selling Strychnine,* August, 2013, Narda Robinson DO, DVM, Colorado State University School of Veterinary Medicine.

Our pet food companies keep buying questionable ingredients from China, other countries, and rendering plant products in the U.S., even after continuous contamination problems keep emerging. Who knows what's going into your pet's stomach?

You would think the pet food industry would have had an epiphany after the China/melamine disaster. Not so. Recently, in 2019, the U.S. Food and Drug Administration alerted the public about the increasing cases of DCM, dilated-cardiomyopathy (over 500 cases known—who knows how many really?), that certain brands of "grain-free" pet foods are linked to. The FDA actually specifically named 16 pet food brands connected to the disease. And these brands are all considered "high-end."

Grain-free foods are the latest fad in pet food consumerism and marketing. But, instead of grain they use peas, lentils, legume seeds, and potatoes as their primary ingredients. Who knows what bizarre combination of contaminants are in those ingredients?

The Pet Food Institute (a trade group representing 98% of pet foods) said about the DCM-causing brands, **"This is a complex issue with many factors requiring scientific evaluation and may be the result of many factors, including recipe formulation and processing."**

WELL, DUH! Maybe if the industry didn't use over-processed byproducts, and stuff that no one knows what it is, except for "scientists," we wouldn't be having this problem!

The pet food industry's **only oversight** is AAFCO (Association of American Feed Control Officials). It is a voluntary organization with **no regulatory or legal authority** to police the pet food industry. It only "advises." Basically, all it really does is provide definitions for the industrial byproducts commonly used as ingredients in pet foods.[2] The U.S. government gets involved if there is a problem (maybe); not to prevent problems.

The FDA alerted the public about the dilated cardio-myopathy from grain-free foods, but did not do that until hundreds of pets

---

2 See Appendix 1.

died, and only after massive veterinary community insistence.

Mass-produced pet foods rely on food ingredients of **variable or unknown quality**. They use literally mountains of ingredients. Pet foods are often formulated with ingredient choices based on cost and availability rather than quality. The **analysis** on the pet food label can remain constant, but the nutrient **quality** of the protein and other sources in the food may **fluctuate** significantly. (Hard to believe, but pet food manufacturers don't have to change the label on their food for six months after they change ingredients.)

Most pet food companies do *not* use *whole foods* as ingredients— that is vegetables and grains in their original form, grown in fertile soil, and harvested without refinement, that contain a complex array of essential nutrients, enzymes, phytochemicals, and antioxidants to support health. In fact, companies use byproducts that would otherwise be used as fertilizer!

The "meat" ingredients used are generally **not fit for human consumption** or worse, they can be products from the rendering industry, including "4D" carcasses (**diseased, dead, dying, disabled**).

Instead of whole foods, the pet food industry is using leftover ingredients from industrial processing often of uncertain origin, quality, and safety; and those ingredients come from all over the world with **no regulation** whatsoever. It is not unusual for these ingredients to have already been **processed** with heat, solvents, and chemicals **4 to 6 times** before the pet food company runs them through their **multiple processes again,** to make kibble, or can it.

Do *not* eat dog and cat food!

CHAPTER 1

THE (SCARY) PET FOOD INDUSTRY

You don't have to be a scientist to cook for your pet, but you have to be a scientist to cook for a pet food company.
Making commercial pet food is like you trying to make a meatloaf tonight out of beet pulp, animal digest, beef tallow, linseed meal, reduced lactose whey, and peanut hulls.

Commercial pet food manufacture is a "science" because they use pieces and parts of foods combining them to make something "complete-and-balanced," or "whole" again. (Frankenfood?)

Where did the idea come from that it is better to feed soy, corn, and wheat gluten forms of protein to a dog instead of meat? Where did the idea come from that you can't feed your pet what you eat because it is bad for them? Why do we actually feel guilty about sharing our food with our pets because it's supposed to somehow be bad for them? That's just silly. Dogs have lived with us sharing (and hunting for) our food for thousands of years. Cats were "mousers."

The commercial pet food industry has convinced us that feeding dogs and cats is too difficult for us to manage. Well, it would be if you used what they use.

Pet food manufacturers may be the only market for industrial ingredients that otherwise would be used for fertilizer, livestock feed, or thrown away.[3] Considering the ingredients they work with it is amazing what they accomplish. They have found a use for many abundant agricultural byproducts from around the world. It takes a huge infrastructure to process these ingredients into edible pet food: chemistry, cooking, extruding, spraying, shaping, coloring, preserving, texturing, hydrating, dehydrating, packaging, shipping, storage, and eventually retailing. You have to hand it to them; it is amazing the millions of animals they feed daily.

Many brands are made by "ghost" factories. Competitors' brands are often made in the same plant. The only difference between two brands may be just insignificant percentages of ingredients, or just the bag itself.[4]

Contrary to the culturally entrenched paradigm that says you are not qualified to make pet food (largely created by pet food manufacturers), the truth is that you can make homemade food for your pets cheaply and easily. You don't have to feed your pet commercially prepared food. And you don't have to use ingredients that you have never heard of.

And this is **unbelievable**: Pet food manufacturers may not even feed their product to an actual animal for testing. There are very few companies that actually do "feeding-trials." And if they do, the feeding-trial guidelines they are supposed to adhere to are ridiculously shallow and unsophisticated.[5] Instead of really testing their products on actual animals, it is your pet that is the "test animal!" (Your pet is doing a fifteen-year feeding-trial.)[6]

3 Feeding livestock is very different than feeding a pet. The long-term effects of ingredients are not considered when the animal raised for food is slaughtered at a young age, whereas pets live into old age. Besides, cattle's digestive systems rely on huge bacterial populations to ferment or "digest" the food first—then the bacteria are digested by the animal.

4 See Chapter 9, on how to read pet food labels.

5 See Chapter 9 for AAFCO feeding trial guidelines.

6 Some companies do maintain populations in the hundreds of animals that have been fed their foods through all life stages. Many of these dogs and cats are treated extremely well for their whole life in that kennel environment. Generally, these colonies are closed to the public.

Instead of using industrial byproducts as ingredients, you can use real whole foods: chicken, turkey, hamburger, oatmeal, cornmeal, rice, noodles, pasta, vegetables, whole eggs, salmon filets, pot roast, cheese, spinach—really anything you eat.[7]

You don't have to know about dry matter, digestible energy, resistant starch, oligosaccharides, nitrogen-free extract, the biological dose-response curve of nutrients, bioavailability, etc.

An egg is balanced, complete, and whole—it's going to be a whole live chicken someday, so it literally has everything, in the right proportions, that it needs for life. So, scramble up some eggs for your pet. Add some cheese, meat, butter or milk, and some peas or carrots. You can't tell me that's not good for a pet. (Wild animals love eggs, shell and all.)

Cats have evolved over thousands of years to be highly skilled predators. They are strict carnivores (meat eaters). They cannot even digest carbohydrates. Yet, we feed them corn...pretty much all carbs? (Imagine "vegan" panthers hunting for corn on the cob!)

You have to wonder: If pet food producers all use the same ingredients, why is **their** brand boasted as the "best"? There is a new brand, type, stage, or flavor introduced daily—literally a 1000 in the last three years. How can they all be the best? With over 15,000 different brands, styles, snacks, flavors, and stages, what is the consumer to do? Their marketing departments will tell you what to do.

A company's sales relate directly to the amount of shelf space they occupy at the grocery store—hence the need for more flavors, more stages, more "specialization." The products are often identical except for a tiny amount of flavoring, which the pet either doesn't care about, or even notice. (It's the same for toothpaste.) Retailers are afraid not to stock them all, or you will go somewhere else after being hammered by advertising (marketing).

The labels on pet foods mean very little and in fact are

---

7 See Chapter 4 for a list of things pets can't eat.

misleading. We will devote an entire chapter on what to look for in commercially prepared pet food, and all the things the marketing departments say…that don't mean anything.[8]

The pet food industry (and veterinary medicine) since the 1950s has contributed to the healthiest, most long-lived population of domestic pets in the history of mankind. Even using industrial leftover ingredients, pet food manufacturers have largely been an incredible and undeniable success. We have ease of use, consistency, and the stuff just doesn't spoil. It is rare that it makes pets sick. Commercial pet foods are energy dense, efficient, and affordable. Many of us wouldn't even have pets if it wasn't for the pet food industry making it so easy to feed them. Cook for my dog, you say? Really?! I don't even cook for myself! (Maybe you should!)

But…there is a lot of hype, propaganda, and even outright deception committed by the pet food industry. Pet food companies want to make you feel good about feeding their brands by informing you that they are premium, natural, organic, for all life-stages, new and improved, meets or exceeds, joint protecting, hairball cleansing, teeth cleaning, wild grown, range fed, great tasting, new and even greater tasting, appeals to their wild side, human grade, fiber enhanced, fun, exciting, and so on…ad-nauseum. (Fun and exciting? Give me a break.) Not one of these claims is backed up by any legal document or authority—they are all literally meaningless.

Don't they understand all this is ludicrous? *"It's difficult to get someone to understand something when his salary depends upon his not understanding it."* –Upton Sinclair, *The Jungle*; an exposé of the meatpacking industry in 1906.

They even sue each other. (Or just buy each other out.) Purina has sued Blue Buffalo for false advertising, commercial disparagement, and unjust enrichment. Purina claims an outside lab found that Blue Buffalo's no-poultry-byproduct meal claim wasn't true; their product *Life Protection* was one-quarter byproduct

---

8 See Chapter 9, on how to read pet food labels.

meal. Blue Buffalo claimed their product didn't have melamine during the Chinese melamine recall and pounced on Purina for their "negligence." But it did have melamine; Blue Buffalo had to pull a third of its product line because of it (quietly). Blue Buffalo accused Purina of "voodoo" science. Purina says Blue Buffalo is built on lies. Blue Buffalo stresses that it is family run, but is actually owned by a big Wall Street firm and they outsource all their manufacturing. (Until just recently Blue Buffalo did not own a manufacturing facility.) Purina insists that Blue Buffalo's key ingredient claims aren't true, and that they have a history of exaggerating what their products do.

Purina proclaims in ads: "Taste that makes mealtime sensational!" "The specialized formula that's just right for your dog!" "Optimal nutrient absorption throughout your dog's body!" "We formulate our food with real meat, poultry, or fish to increase bioavailability!"

Blue Buffalo says: "Provides essential phytonutrients, antioxidants, and enzymes!" "Cold formed to retain their potency!" "Life Source bits!" "Selected by holistic veterinarians and animal nutritionists!"

What B.S.

Blue Buffalo was bought by General Mills "catapulting G.M. into the growing market for pet foods made with what it calls 'wholesome" ingredients." I wouldn't call it wholesome at all. At a veterinary conference I attended I stopped by the Blue Buffalo booth. This was when Blue Buffalo was new. I asked the factory rep, "What is so great about your food?" He said, and I kid you not, "We add kelp and blueberries." Seriously…that's all he had to say!

You and I could start a pet food company this weekend using our bathtub, and no one can tell us what to put in our "secret formula," which we can claim to be "the best." There are no laws, no licenses needed, no standards required, no regulations to follow, and as stated before, no governmental oversight to worry about (other than tax laws, zoning laws, laws governing the conduct of business, etc.). We can say anything we want about our pet food. It may be made out of crank case oil, shoe leather, charcoal, and crushed limestone, but the label can boast that it is "fully balanced and complete." After you and I have made our brand of pet food, we can pitch it with testimonials like: *I've been around dogs all my life; I've raised, trained, and shown labs all my life; my pets have never been healthier; you can see the difference; a leading pet food expert agrees; it's preservative free* (is that actually a good thing?); *it has pre-pro and syn-biotics;* etc. We can start small using a generic-contract manufacturer to make the stuff for us. Slap on a label and come up with a good slogan. Add kelp and blueberries and call those "Life Source Bits." That's what Blue Buffalo did.

The nutritional standard for decades has been that of addressing deficiencies—or what scientists call "essentiality"; that is, the supplying of missing key vitamins, minerals, amino acids, trace nutrients, etc. Pets did have deficiencies like that years ago, and the pet food industry scientists made great contributions there. But a new nutritional standard is emerging now that shows that many ingredients can actually be harmful, that it isn't enough anymore to be complete and balanced, and that it isn't enough anymore that it just gives your pet the energy it needs to make its heart beat, toenails grow, and come when you call it. It also has to do no harm, cause no cancer, cause no kidney disease, not cause diabetes, not contribute to allergic dermatitis, not cause dilated cardiomyopathy, and not cause long-term side effects. Consumers are becoming wary.

This new paradigm shift also finds that some nutrients can be beneficial at levels greater than may be required as a minimum essential. It also finds that too much of a good thing might not be a good thing (like too much fat, or vitamin A, or D). There is a *quality* issue now.

Interestingly, manufacturers are starting to meet the demands of the new well-informed consumer looking for quality. Just advertising that your food is balanced and complete doesn't hack it anymore. The consumer is showing that they are willing to pay for quality, and that they are seeing though the propaganda. Because of the cost of better ingredients, it is not unusual to see specialty pet foods selling for three times the amount paid for the typical grocery store brands. People are trying to eat healthy—they want their pets to eat healthy too.

Commercial pet foods have way too many carbohydrates for our carnivorous pets. Carbs (grains) are cheap, but they aren't any better for pets than they are for us (as the primary ingredient). When they tout being "grain free" now that doesn't mean that there is more meat—it means they are using potatoes and peas instead of grain. Additionally additives abound, such as: artificial flavors, "digest" sprayed on for flavor enhancement, artificial colors and dyes, preservatives, taste and texture enhancers, thickeners, fiber (which is cellulose—literally paper!), humectants (glycerin), enzyme inhibitors, tannins, oxalates, glycosylates, phytates, estrogens, alkaloids, genetically modified materials, irradiated materials, melamine, urea, and on and on.

A Frito-Lay Cheeto without its powdered coating has almost no flavor. Sauces on processed convenience foods allow a common chicken base, which has almost no flavor, to be used as a common base for two or three different sauces for a full product line.

One key to getting pets, that are not grain eaters by choice, to eat cheap grain-based diets, is the application of topical liquid and dry flavor systems known as "palatants." Enter AFB International Research and Development, a company that makes flavor coatings for pet foods. Liquid palatants are delivered in bulk tankers. Kibble is extruded, fat is applied, then an AFB, liquid or dry, palatant is applied.

Sodium acid pyrophosphate (SAPP) is part if the founding patent for AFB International. Pyrophosphates have been described as "cat crack." Coat some kibble with it and a cat will eat pretty much anything. (It takes a scientist.)

Pet food companies love palatants. As one AFB employee put

it, "The client can go, 'Here's my product. I want to cut corners here and here and here, and I want you to cover up all the sins.'" This is especially doable with dog food, as dogs rely more on smell than taste. If the palatant smells appealing, the dog will dive in and the owner sees the food is a winner, but it may have only smelled like a winner.

By the way, colored pet-food pieces (which mean nothing to a dog or cat) that were popular during the 90's, are largely gone because vomit with green and red dye left a stained carpet.

Then there are the mint-flavored treats shaped like a toothbrush. Mint is an irritant less than a flavor which may explain the vomiting.

Things such as fertilizers, pest control products, antibiotics, and other chemical residues can concentrate during multiple processing. Even the coatings inside the bag may potentially contribute to this toxic residue. Many toxins found in pet food are not actually added by the pet food companies. They are already there in the ingredients they use. The pet food manufacturer may not even know about them. Even if they do know about them, since they didn't add them, they are not required to list them on the label. Pet foods that are supposedly preservative free may contain ingredients that have preservatives in them that the pet food manufacturer may or may not know about. Manufacturers do not have to disclose ingredients that they themselves did not add to their final product.

The *Association of American Feed Control Officials* (AAFCO) has drawn up guidelines with definitions of ingredients used in pet food production. (See Appendix 1 for the complete list.) But these AAFCO definitions can be interpreted by pet food companies to their desires. For instance, the AAFCO definition for "beef and bone meal" is: *The rendered product from beef tissues, including bone, exclusive of any **added** blood, hair, hoof, horn, hide trimmings, manure, stomach and rumen[9] contents, except in such*

---

9 Cows and sheep have four stomachs. The first one is called the rumen. It is a large "fermentation vat" where cellulose (grass, hay, etc.) is digested by bacterial action. Humans, dogs, and cats cannot

amounts as may occur unavoidable in good processing practices.
This does **not** mean that blood, hair, hoof, horn, hide trimmings,
manure, and stomach and rumen contents are **not** present. It just
means they are not supposed to add more.

There is no way for you to tell the difference between what
different manufactures use as "chicken byproducts." For instance, has
the byproduct been purchased from a rendering company? How
was this ingredient handled at the slaughterhouse, during transport?

Is beef-and-bone-meal full of drugs and antibiotics, and
whatever else the farmer desperately gave the poor animal during
its dying days? How long was it dead, was it winter or summer,
were there flies and maggots all over it, poisonous plant material in
it, snakebite venom, hoof and mouth disease, tuberculosis, cancer,
etc.? Or is the xylazine, ketamine, and Pentothal cocktail the vet
used to euthanize the poor animal still in it?

It is up to the discretion of the manufacturer where their
ingredients come from. Does it come from carefully slaughtered
animals, or from the rendering plant, or from sources declared
unfit for human consumption?

By the way, just who is going to strip the feces out of a bloated
maggot-infested cow that's been dead for four days, so that you
can be sure feces isn't in your dog's food? (The maggots may be
the most nutritious part, by the way!)

The U.S. Coast Guard requires any fish meal not destined
for human consumption to be preserved with ethoxyquin. It is
used to prevent rancidity. (It is also used as a pesticide and as a
hardening agent in the manufacture of rubber.) There is an ongoing
controversy surrounding the use of ethoxyquin. It finds its way
into pet foods using fish meal.

The rendering industry soaks carcasses in carbolic acid,
citronella oil, fuel oil, and other chemicals to denature them and
insure they won't be used for human food. These chemicals do

---

digest cellulose. That's why cows are so useful. They convert the inedible to edible for a human.

not necessarily break down and disappear with high temperature cooking and steaming by pet food companies. Residues remain all the way to the feed bowl. (And we wonder why things like cardiomyopathy occur in our pets?!)

No matter how much the pet food manufacturer's marketing department tries to convince you of the high quality of their ingredients, the truth is most of the nutritious parts have already been extracted from the ingredients they use. There is really nothing nutritious left of the tomato after ketchup is extracted from it.

If you are feeding a commercial pet food you really are at the mercy of the manufacturer and their marketing people. Seemingly innocuous pet foods may include too much fat leading to obesity; poor-quality protein leading to kidney disease; too may carbs leading to diabetes; tasty coatings leading to overeating; fiber-filler leading to offensive gas production; contaminants from impure ingredients; preservatives, dyes, and fractions of foods that are highly allergenic; mold leading to G.I. upsets; ground-up fish and poultry carcasses causing too much ash contributing to urinary tract stones; too many carbohydrates resulting in an alkaline urine instead of acidic, making the animal more prone to bladder infections; complex junky proteins causing dermatitis, and on and on.

It's not nice to fool Mother Nature.

So, industrially manufactured mass-produced commercial pet food may be "complete and balanced" (actually not really), and prevent every single possible nutritional deficiency (actually not really), and supplies all minimums (we aren't certain what those minimums are, by the way), but that doesn't make the food healthy and wholesome. In fact, it may be doing harm. But it's easy and affordable to buy and feed, it lasts forever, and we feel good about feeding it (thanks, marketing).

In conclusion: There is no one looking over pet food manufacturers' shoulders. They use peculiar strange stuff as ingredients. Some of those ingredients are far from wholesome or healthy. Much of what they say about their foods is fabrication, or literally untruth. Many brands use the same ingredients and therefore are alike. But they feed the world's millions of pets every day. Their scientists do an amazing job with what they've got to work with. For that we are truly grateful. They just don't feed my pets anymore. I cook for mine.

Permission for Williams to use cartoon in print/electronic.

CHAPTER 2

WHAT TO LOOK FOR WHEN SELECTING COMMERCIAL PET FOOD

Cooking for your pet may be out of the question. You might not even have a pet if you had to cook for him or her. Maybe you don't cook for yourself. You may not even have a kitchen. Maybe you eat every meal out. Or microwave something highly processed every night yourself.

But there is no doubt that feeding your pet dry kibble, of all the available commercial foods, is the furthest removed from food in its natural state possible, because of the ingredients used, and the many layers of processing necessary to make it.

But you want to open the bag, fill the bowl, done deal. You trust Corporate America and the world's food supply chain. Of course, you don't want it to make your pet sick and vomit, or gassy, or cause diarrhea. You want your pet to come running like they do on TV when you holler "dinner." The price is important. The human-animal bond is now complete. You can go on about your business knowing "everything is in the bag—just add water." You know because *marketing told you so.*

Here are the guidelines to follow when choosing a commercial pet food:

1. The LARGE companies have a lot to lose if they make pets sick. They do have fastidious production processes. They do have quality control mechanisms in place. It's probably safest to stay with a large well-known manufacturer. The small manufacturer may believe strongly in the nutritional value of kelp or grapes (not kidding). Besides, the large companies, because of their excellent purchasing organizations, often have first dibs on the higher-quality ingredients.

2. Look for an 800-number on the bag or a website. Call them and ask if they have a nutritionist with a university degree on staff. Check the website for information on their nutritional research and oversight team. Their nutritionists' credentials shouldn't just be "I've raised and shown dogs my whole life" or "All fifteen of my dogs have never been healthier" or "Blueberries are a natural antioxidant and saved my dog's life." You get the picture.

3. Look for a company that actually maintains a population of animals that eat their food under the observation of a nutritionist that studies such things as absorbability, digestibility, interaction with other ingredients, etc. Some large companies take feeding trials seriously and have their own thorough protocols and maintain populations of animals for testing.

4. On the label watch for: *formulated according to standards* or *formulated to meet a profile.* Who knows what/whose standards they mean? This also means the diet has probably never been fed to a dog or cat in a controlled feeding trial. So, your pet is the test animal.

5. It needs to be labeled: *complete and balanced.* If the label says *intended for use as an intermittent or supplemental diet* it is not complete and balanced, so not intended for continuing use.

6. These are diets may have been formulated for a specific therapy such as dissolving certain types of bladder stones. (The stones caused by feeding their food?)

7. Be **skeptical** of all marketing jargon. For instance, the terms ***organic, human grade, premium, holistic*** have zero meaning, or a definition, in the pet food industry—as in, not established by the USDA (United States Department of Agriculture). These terms are grossly overused and assigned much more meaning than they actually have.

8. The term ***natural*** just means there are no chemically synthesized ingredients in it (which is something good, I guess?). If it says ***natural-with,*** then preservatives can be added (which kind of negates the whole concept of natural, doesn't it?). By the way, the term *natural* has not been established by the USDA for human food.

9. In human food the term ***organic*** means only that there are no pesticides, growth hormones, or sewage-sludge in the ingredient, but this is already regulated anyway industry-wide by the USDA so those things aren't supposed to be in our food supply anyway. This term is grossly overused and assigned much more meaning than it actually has. There are "organic-certified" farms.[10] But most pet food manufacturers cannot meet

---

10 Internet search: "USDA Agriculture Marketing Service's National Organic Program." Organic farming uses methods such as crop rotation, soil enrichment by plowing under soil nutrient-providing crops such as clover; the use of large quantities of compost; the use of non-genetically modified seeds; no chemical pesticides; etc. It is extremely difficult to comply with the myriad of rules and guidelines mandated for true organic farming. Products from true organic farming are worth it if you can be sure they really are from such a farm, and not just marketing hype.

their supply demands from these facilities. (Actually, there is a very popular fertilizer available that is made of sewage-sludge. People spread it on their lawns and dogs just love to eat it.)

10. ***Free range*** is another marketing deception. When interviewing a chicken farmer who raises chickens for a huge company he admitted (chuckling) that "free-range" only means having a door open with a small fenced area available at the end of the chicken house (that has thousands of chickens in it). He said they never go out the door. But they could if they wanted to. (Eyes roll, smirk, elbow, elbow.)

11. Some pet owners think of grain as "filler." Not necessarily true. Whole grains are an excellent and economical source of useful protein, fat, and carbohydrates. "Fractions" of grains, as mentioned before, may not be such a great source of nutrition as all that may be left may be starch. The fat (vegetable oil) and protein (gluten) may be gone. Just carbs (starch) are left. So, they add fat and protein from another source—usually of poorer quality than the original content.

12. All commercially prepared pet foods use ***byproducts.*** Byproducts are not necessarily bad. In fact, a few generations ago, there were no such things as byproducts because everything from the animal was used after slaughter: kidneys, liver, brains, tongues, glands, etc. The fat was rendered to lard. The feet were pickled. The testicles were fried (Rocky Mountain Oysters). Cooked pancreas was called "sweet breads." Ox tails were made into soup. Intestines made into sausage casings. A lot of these excellent quality foodstuffs are called "byproducts" now because humans no longer consume them, and so they find their way into pet food. But most of the byproducts used in pet food are not parts of animals that humans don't eat anymore. They are left-over from industrial processing.

13. Many pet food manufacturers use *rendered* **animal tissues**. The rendering industry processes products not used for human consumption and produce around ten billion pounds annually of useable ingredients for the pet food industry as well as for medicines, makeup, etc. What is that source of protein in that bag of dog food you're feeding? You can be sure it's not beef tenderloin. Not boned chicken breasts. Not porkchops. Not ground chuck. It can be anything from anywhere. But not necessarily bad. For instance, animal muscle protein bits harvested from beef fat trimmings is pure beef skeletal muscle and is added to hamburger for human consumption to increase the protein content. (There is nothing wrong with "pink slime"—as one journalist called it.) But the protein in your pet's food could be from the rendering industry. Look up "rendering" on the internet. It is an unbelievably huge industry. I don't want to eat the stuff, so I don't like feeding it to my dog. (Your French fries may be cooked in rendered oil.)

14. Select the appropriate life stage which should be substantiated by the company's feeding trials (or it may just be meaningless marketing jargon). For instance, the term *senior diet* **is meaningless**. It is really just an "adult diet." It may have added fiber (paper/wood…as in cellulose) in it as a result of somebody's notion that old dogs are prone to constipation, or tend toward obesity, so need fewer calories per bite. (Actually, this may be detrimental to the older dog that may need all the energy per bite he can get.) Dogs don't need fiber like we do. Instead of feeding "senior diet" just feed your old dog the best adult dog food you can find, or even puppy food if they are losing weight. And table food.

15. When considering which pet food to buy, ask the question, is the animal able to do its job on the food selected—hunting, seeing-eye work, guard work, etc.?

16. When feeding kibble, moisten it with warm water or broth. It makes food easier to digest, increases fluid intake, reduces the body's need to provide fluid for digestion, and it reduces the dry kibble's astringent/inflammatory effect on the stomach.

17. If you add a large portion of canned food to the daily intake much of the harm potential of the kibble-only diet is minimized.

18. If you are willing to add fresh animal protein daily in the form of meat, dairy products, eggs, etc. you will even further enhance your pet's nutritional health.

19. Feed cats canned wet foods is a priority. (See the chapter on cat feeding.)

20. Vary brands of food fed. Research brands. Well-put-together pet food lines are sometimes the victim of their own success. They start switching ingredients because of supply problems and cost. Many get gobbled up by large companies who change the formula. Almost every brand I recommended twenty years ago has been bought up by a multinational conglomerate. I am convinced those brands are not what they used to be. With consumer trends going toward specialty foods every giant pet food company has launched a so-called "premium brand" named and labeled and marketed as if it was not part of the conglomerate even though it is made in the same plant using largely the same ingredients as their regular food.

21. The terms **high-protein** and **high-pro** **are meaningless**, and not established by the USDA or AAFCO. In fact, a diet can be too high in protein, or have such poor-quality protein that it can be detrimental to the animal's kidneys. (Remember melamine from China that was used to artificially inflate the protein content.)

22. The **first three ingredients on the package label should be from an animal source,** as opposed to a grain source. Remember, the first ingredient may be meat, but if the next three are grain then the total amount of grain per bite probably outweighs the total meat—usually by a significant ratio.

23. If the label says *with catfish* that means it has to have only 3% catfish in it. (What part of the catfish? That is up to the manufacturer.) If it says *fish flavor* that only means that that particular flavor can be distinguished. (Your cat is thinking, "You got to be kidding me!") By the way, fish is not a natural diet for cats. Thanks, marketing.

24. The term *guaranteed analysis* **on the pet food label has nothing to do with what the actual ingredients are in the food.** It tells only the **minimum** amount of fat and protein in the food, not the **actual** amount—so it could have lots more fat than the "minimum." Fat is always a good flavor enhancer…and cheap…and often in unhealthy excess in commercial pet (and human) foods. For instance, within one brand of cat food, the fat content varies from 25% fat to 55% depending on the variety/flavor. That's a LOT of fat! There is no way to tell which one has the higher fat because the label just gives the minimum amount, not the actual amount.

25. The *guaranteed analysis* on the label of pet food lists only the maximum amount of fiber and moisture in the food. The amount of protein may look adequate in a dry food, but if you were to add as much water to the dry food as found in a similar canned version, there may actually be less protein per bite.

26. The terms *light, lite, reduced, low-calorie, weight-reduction* mean very little because what is "light" for one brand may still be higher in calories than another brand's "regular" diet. A

manufacturer can reduce from 600 calories to 500 calories per measure and call it "reduced" but may still have more calories than another brand that only has 400 calories per measure in its food anyway. (All the pet has to do to reduce calories is eat less.) The calorie count is rarely on the label. The calorie count may not even be consistent from batch to batch.

27. **A shiny hair coat, or a good stool consistency, doesn't mean the food you are feeding is good for your pet, or even balanced.** It may actually indicate that the product has too much fat giving the shiny coat. Or a good stool may indicate that the product contains lots of indigestible fiber (cellulose—paper).

28. The bottom line is: **You pretty much get what you pay for in the pet food industry.** The quality of the ingredients drives the cost of the food. More expensive ingredients—more expensive food. **Bargain foods may not be as digestible or as absorbable as more costly foods, thereby negating any savings you might think you achieved by buying the cheaper food.** The pet just eats more of it. Cheaper food often results in larger stools and flatulence too (poor digestibility). Additionally, cheap ingredients may not allow normal development if fed to a growing animal.

That's a lot of work, sorting through 26 things, isn't it? Quality may even vary from bag to bag and batch to batch! Then there is shipping and storage in hot semi-trailers, warehouses, and boxcars. What happens when canned food is frozen?

What's worse, as said before, is that once you find a brand you trust, the manufacturer may change the ingredients on you. Excellent brands are being bought by huge conglomerates that then change the formulas and ingredients, with impunity, and with no notice. Proctor & Gamble purchased the *Iams Company,* which manufactured the trusted *Eukanuba* brand. Shortly after purchase, P&G expanded the line, making it available everywhere as opposed to specialty stores and veterinary clinics as it had originally been. Soon, it became apparent there had been changes made as dogs came down with diarrhea, intense itching, brittle hair coats, rashes, etc.

After a huge public reaction P&G admitted switching from rice to barley in *Eukanuba*. They claimed that was an "enhancement." Iams and Eukanuba has subsequently lost favor as a "premium" brand.

P&G was sued (pet food companies sue each other all the time) by *Nutro* and *Kal Kan* pet food companies for false advertising and misleading labels on Iams and Eukanuba. Plus, there was a class action lawsuit on behalf of consumers that proved *Iams* and *Eukanuba* had changed ingredients to the detriment of their pet's health. The suits were settled out of court. Who knows what the truth of it all was? Some scientist (retired on the beach?) does somewhere.

I am not offering this as an exposé attempting to blame and shame Procter & Gamble, or Iams, or scientists. My point is to show that pet food manufactures can do whatever they want with their formulas and ingredients in their products. There are no laws against it. They don't even have to change the labels. Buyer beware, and all that.

There is no evil giant corporate conspiracy to poison all the dogs in the world for profit. I think pet food companies are doing the absolute best they can with what they've got. They are highly exposed and accountable. It's an insanely competitive price-driven market. They don't want to cause disease and death (it's bad for business, if for no other reason). I think it's amazing that they put out as good a product as they do. Commercial pet food production is certainly a herculean, colossal, and staggering achievement. They are literally feeding the world's dogs and cats.

The pet food industry is a huge business with marketing and advertising driving the show, with vast worldwide ingredient and transportation contracts, with continuous changes of ingredients being made due to market availability and economic pressures, with giant factories and thousands of employees (and scientists), stewardship issues of shareholders' investments, legal issues, tax issues, and on and on. I know I could never run a pet food company.

But:

- Your pet is part of your pet food company's field trial colony.
- They tweak their formulas regularly, not to make it better, but to adjust to ingredient availability or costs.
- The label claims on the bag of your pet's food that it is organic, natural, human-grade, premium, free-range, holistic, high-pro, senior, and fish/chicken/whatever-flavor...all mean little to nothing. (Thanks, marketing.)
- There is usually little to none of "whole-foods" in most commercial factory produced pet food.
- Even the really good brands often get bought up and their formulas changed, and probably not for the good.
- Your pet may be eating "rendered" animal ingredients... certainly not what you would be buying at the meat counter.
- Your pet will be eating byproducts/leftovers/unfit-for-human-consumption ingredients from some manufacturing process that maybe from some other part of the world where regulation is completely nonexistent.
- Dry kibble is as far from what a dog or cat would eat historically as possible.
- Commercial pet food is full of chemicals.
- The terms light, weight-reduction, and weight-loss mean absolutely nothing.
- The label's list of ingredients is misleading.
- The label's guaranteed analysis means nothing.
- There is no government regulation or oversight for the pet food industry.
- Okay, it's convenient, and cheap.

Again, I cook for my pets. I make my own pet food out of what I would also eat.

CHAPTER 3

PET FOOD LABELS

Don't expect to be able to interpret much from of the label. They can be very misleading, in fact (on purpose?).

The only thing of any value on the label is the *list of ingredients.* That's useful to try to make sure certain things **aren't in there**.

Look for a list of ingredients that you can recognize as whole food instead of leftover parts of foods that you have to look up to get an idea (sort of) what they actually are.

WHAT YOU SHOULD FIND ON THE LABEL:

1. The label on pet food containers is considered a legal document. It is required:
   - That it has the *manufacturer's name,*
   - That it has the *brand name* or *product name,* which can be a key factor in the consumer's decision to buy it. The manufacturer (marketing) often uses fantastic fanciful names to emphasize certain ingredients whether they are in there in reasonable quantity or not. (See below.)
   - It should say whether it is dog or cat food,
   - It should have its *net weight,*

- It should have a *designator* of what it is basically made out of (i.e. tuna, 95%; tuna and shrimp, 75% and 25%; with catfish, 3%; etc.).

2. The label has nothing to do at all with what the *quality* of the ingredients.

3. The label is primarily *advertising*.

4. The label has a backside statement that includes:
   - A nutritional adequacy statement that should say, "Complete and balanced." (Which is a joke—see below.)
   - The label should say how they base their claim that it is complete and balanced. (For instance: Formulated according to an established profile, or through feeding trials—see below.)
   - And the intended life stage.

5. The label has a *Guaranteed Analysis*: This doesn't tell you much. See below.

6. The label has a list of *Ingredients*: They are listed in decreasing order by weight. But not weight as that ingredient is now in the bag, but by its weight before processing (with the water still in it), and before putting it in the bag. I'll explain why that is misleading below.

7. The label has *Feeding Directions*: Manufacturers seem to have a goal of selling more food, which results in overfeeding. Imagine that?

8. The label may have a *Calorie Statement*: This is not mandated unfortunately. Few companies voluntarily add it. It used to be against AAFCO rules to add it, believe it or not.

If calorie content per measure is on the label it is useful for weight loss programs. But the calories per bag actually vary considerably, so the claim would be a "range" anyway.

9. The label may have other label claims such as the terms premium, natural, organic, human grade, holistic, etc., which are just meaningless marketing tools.

LET'S PICK THE LABEL APART:
*The pet food label's *guaranteed analysis* doesn't tell us anything about quality (or much about quantity either).

"Protein" could be shoe leather…or roast beef (not) or something in between including rendered sources (dead, diseased, disabled, dying—the "4-Ds"). Fat could be in there in any quantity and from any source. Some varieties by the same brand differ in fat content as much as 100%. The guaranteed analysis gives only the *minimum* content of protein and fat. So that real amount of fat and protein can vary upward. *That means there can be more fat in there than they say.*

On the other hand, the guaranteed analysis gives the *maximum* amount of moisture and fiber in the food *so that can vary downward.* Like less moisture than is printed on the bag.

Other ingredients may also be listed but are not required. If you want a list of actual "other ingredients," the company should be able to provide that to you, such as percent of ash, magnesium, calcium, etc.

It doesn't tell us much, does it?

*The pet food label's *brand name* or *product name* can be misleading. There are some AAFCO guidelines the label is supposed to follow, but remember, AAFCO has no enforcement power to force manufacturers to follow their guidelines. They use the honor system. (Besides, I think their guidelines are ambiguous and misleading.)

- If the food is specifically named on the label "Beef Dog Food," it has to be composed of beef not less than 95% of its weight excluding water[11], according to AAFCO guidelines. If it says "Beef and Liver Dog Food," it has to be not less than 95% beef and liver excluding the water. This level of protein is usually found only in canned food. By the way, just what is the quality of the beef? Absolutely no telling. (See Appendix 1.)
- If the pet food name includes the words "dinner, formula, nuggets," such as "Lamb Formula," then it has to have not less than 25% of its weight as lamb, excluding water, according to AAFCO guidelines. If it says "Lamb and Rice," the combined amount of lamb and rice must be not less than 25%, excluding water.

Again, this has nothing to do with quality. Since the named ingredient only has to be 25% lamb and rice, then the other 75% can be anything such as corn, soy, rice, etc. So, in these dog foods the descriptive brand name may not be at all descriptive of what the actual main ingredient is—not actually lamb—but grain in reality.

So, as an example: "Lamb and Rice Formula" might be *ground corn, wheat middlings, meat and bone meal, **lamb, rice**....* In this example the main ingredient would be **corn** even though the product may be named "Lamb and Rice Dinner." (Worse than confused by now? Me too.)

- If the pet food name states **"with lamb,"** that means it has to be "not less than 3% lamb." So, if you see "with-lamb, with-beef, with-whatever," that does not describe accurately what is in the bag or can at all. It says that it probably has around 3% lamb

---

11 I have yet to find what "excluding water" means exactly. Does it mean you can't include the water in the protein percentage? Or does it mean the water counts the same as the protein? If it is the latter, then 95% protein could actually be 90% water and 5% protein. Is this ambiguous and misleading? For me, yep.

in the bag. And again, who knows what part of the lamb they are using? It may be anus and ears. I'll bet it isn't lambchops.

- If the pet food name includes the word "flavor" or "flavored-with," there is no specific AAFCO recommended amount or percentage required to be in the bag or can; there only has to be an "amount sufficient to be able to be detected." So, if you buy a pet food that says, "...with liver flavor!" that quantity of liver (it may be *digest of beef liver,* by the way*)* may be way behind the tallow, peanut hulls, corn gluten, poultry byproduct, and brewer's rice. Even though you think you're buying something made out of liver, you're not. (My Labrador is not discerning enough to turn her nose up if she can't detect liver in the food that says it is "flavored-with" liver.) Is this misleading? Definitely.

- And finally, pet food companies are not required to list ingredient changes on pet food labels for 6 months! Wow!

*The pet food label's *ingredient list "in-order-by-weight"* can be misleading as to actual percentages of ingredients in the product as fed from the bag:

If the first ingredient on the list says lamb, you would assume that that would be the most plentiful ingredient in the concoction. But they calculate the "in-order-by-weight" weight of the ingredients *before* they take the water out. In other words, this ingredient list is put together before the moisture in the ingredients is removed. So, the actual weight of lamb in the food may have shrunk to 25% of what it was originally when it was hydrated. If this same concoction used dry chicken meal as another ingredient, which does not shrink much because it is already dry, then it actually may be the primary ingredient in the food. (Really!)

*More on "misleading and ambiguous" pet food labels:

See the AAFCO (Association of American Feed Control Officials) definitions in Appendix 1. You'll have to use your imagination—the descriptions are ambiguous, vague, abstruse, and indefinite. It's like lying by "omission," instead of "commission," frankly.

There are many ingredients used in pet foods that do not have an AAFCO definition. Such things as carrots, peas, spinach, blueberries, etc., aren't defined so we can only speculate as to what form they were in, what contaminants they may contain, and when they were added to the food. These things may be in so small a quantity their effect one way or another is negligible. It may just be for marketing purposes appealing to the pet owner someway. "With blueberries" may mean there is a little blueberry dried powder dusted in. There is no way to know.

Once again, there is no federal regulating agency charged with enforcing the compliance to these vague guidelines set down by AAFCO. At worse, these ingredients may be intentionally adulterated (as in the case of the Chinese melamine-laced gluten). At best the ingredients are what they say they are…but many of which may actually be little more than fertilizer.

AAFCO inadvertently may actually be preventing the consumer from evaluating quality of ingredients by hampering the introduction of better labeling laws. For instance, there is no way to find out if "chicken byproducts" from one manufacturer is better or worse than another's. If the system of the International Feed Name and Number (IFN) were implemented, the accuracy of feed and nutritional information on pet food labels would be positively enhanced.[12] But the AAFCO isn't interested.

---

12 The members of the American Society of Animal Science (the author of this book has a degree in Animal Science as well as the DVM) approved the use of application of the International Feed Name and Number (IFN) system of describing feedstuff. This increases the accuracy of feed and nutritional information described for use in their discipline. It has been suggested that a similar system be used to describe ingredients in pet food. This would allow manufacturers who have taken great effort to use wholesome and toxic free substances to have a way to make it known. At this point there is absolutely no way to surmise quality or detect toxins.

The following is a list of _INGREDIENTS TO AVOID_ in commercial pet foods, and why. If you see any of these ingredients on a label, it's best to move on:

In alphabetical order:

- Animal digest - A material derived from chemical and enzymatic hydrolysis; it is a cooked-down broth made from unspecified parts of unspecified animals. It can be from any kind of animal, including dead, diseased, disabled, or dying (4-D) animals, goats, pigs, horses, rats, roadkill, restaurant/grocery store refuse, and even euthanized animals such as horses put to sleep by veterinarians, then picked up by a rendering service.

- Animal fat - The animal source is not specified. It may not be from "slaughtered" animals. It can be from any kind of animal, including 4-D animals, goats, pigs, horses, rats, roadkill deer, restaurant/grocery store refuse, and euthanized animals.

- Apple pomace - skins, pulp, seeds left over from human food processing. Worthless to a dog or cat.

- Artificial color/dyes - blues, reds, yellows. They are not necessary to encourage a pet to eat. They are ubiquitous in the food industry. Look them up. The chemistry is incredible and complex. Of course, they can cause cancer in mice, but what doesn't? They are just another thing to be allergic to. There is no reason for them in pet food. Some humans react with behavior idiosyncrasies (hyper, aggressive, etc.) to certain dyes, and so do may pets.

- Beef & bone meal - can be good or bad depending on the source. Either way, the quality cuts are always removed so this ingredient includes cuts you may not think of as quality. It can include eyeballs, tails, joints, ears, skulls, salivary glands, bladders (where did the urine go?), prostate glands, intestines/colon/anal sphincters (are they really cleaned out?), spleen, lungs, ears, noses, esophagus, joints, tumors, penis (including the os penis—a bone found in the penis of some species), ovaries and uterus, stomach, ears and anus, and so on. Yum.

- Beef tallow or beef fat - Tasty but another rendered product and missing essential fatty acids. Rendered from the 4-Ds and worse. Lamp oil, I call it.

- BHA and BHT - Antioxidants used to preserve fats and oils. Banned from human use in many countries, but not the U.S. Caused cancer in animal experiments.

- Bone phosphate - A source of phosphorous. From bones processed with hydrochloric acid and lime. Usually used in food animal feed. Steamed bone meal should be used in dogs and cats; it has the natural proper balance of calcium and phosphorous.

- Cane molasses - This is sugar. Completely unnecessary. Pets like it. It can become addictive. It causes mood swings, obesity, tooth decay, arthritis, diabetes, and so on. A little is maybe okay.

- Cellulose - Dried wood. Sawdust. Toilet paper. If you have a pet termite, maybe. It is a fine powder used to add bulk and consistency. It doesn't really do anything at all (bad or good). Just a cheap filler—no nutritional benefit at all. Is used in so-called reduced-calorie pet foods.

- Cereal food fines - Particles of breakfast cereals obtained as a byproduct of their processing. Usually from an unknown source, and of questionable quality, and may contain chemicals, sweeteners, preservatives, dies, etc.

- Chicken byproduct meal - Can be good or bad depending on the source. Either way the quality cuts are removed. So, it is not chicken meat. It is eyes, feet, skulls, undeveloped eggs, intestines, vents, wishbones, the occasional feather, and so on. Who cleans those intestines of chicken poop? I got a feeling some of that gets in there too. Of course, dogs love eating poop…so what?

- Citrus pulp - The dried residue of peel, pulp, and seeds of citrus fruits. It can include twigs and leaves, which may have residues of pesticides, etc., on them. It is usually fed to cattle, but can be used as fiber in pet food. Filler. Worthless to a dog or cat.

- Corn bran - The outer coating of the corn kernel. It is just fiber used to add bulk to pet food. Worthless to dogs and cats.

- Corn cellulose - From the cell walls of corn obtained by a chemical process. It's just fiber to add bulk to pet food. Like cellulose from a tree. Worthless to a dog or cat.

- Corn distillers, dried grains with solubles - Comes from the distilling industry after liquor made from fermentation. It is protein, but it has a high fiber content, is poorly balanced as to its amino acids, and not very digestible. It can vary greatly from batch to batch. Not good stuff for pets.

- Corn germ meal - Left over from the oil extraction process. Okay, it's not a deal killer. It can be rich in protein. It is not harmful, but should not be a primary ingredient.

- Corn gluten and corn gluten meal - It contains some protein. It is a good binding agent. Not inherently harmful, but should not be a main ingredient.

- Corn syrup - Sugar. Should not be in pet foot. Pets like it. Can become addictive. Causes mood swings, obesity, tooth decay, arthritis, diabetes, and so on.

- <u>Digest: chicken-digest; lamb-digest; poultry-liver-digest; animal-digest; poultry-digest</u> - May appear as a dried additive or a flavor-enhancing spray coating. It is residue from unspecific parts of specified, or unspecified animals, that has been rendered by chemical and/or enzymatic hydrolysis. There is no control over contamination or quality. If it is "unspecified" it can come from any kind of animal, in any condition, from any source, from anywhere on the planet. Or even Mars (or Uranus—LOL).

- <u>Ethoxyquin</u> - Used as a post-harvest dip to prevent mold growth on fruit. It is also used as a pesticide for fruit and a color preservative for spices. Originally it was used as a stabilizer for rubber. The original FDA permit for use as a stabilizer in animal feed did not include pet food. It has never been proven safe for the lifespan of dogs and cats. It has been linked to thyroid, kidney, immune related diseases, and cancer. There are studies currently being performed, but until the results are in, the pet food industry may still use it.

- <u>Feeding oat meal</u> - Cattle feed-grade fractioned grain byproduct of human rolled oats processing, and not as nutritional as whole oats. It is broken oat groats, chips, hulls, oat flour, etc.

- <u>Fish meal</u> - Oh, boy…this can be total junk. Like with all animal sources, you never know what the quality it is. There are some fish that people won't eat, but are plentiful and are used in pet food. These usually are whole fish and are a good ingredient. But other sources may be left over from manufacturing after the meat is extracted (tuna, white fish, trout, salmon, etc.). This fish meal may not have much nutrition in it. Fish are being raised commercially all over the world in fish farms and in rivers that are heavily polluted and contaminated. (The Far East, particularly.) The processing is not good either. Plus, the food they use to feed farm-raised fish can literally be feces from other species (still has nutrients in it, but...). The good fish farms use giant netted aqua farms in the self-cleaning ocean. Same problem as many other ingredients used in the pet food industry—quality unknown.

- <u>Flavor</u> - Who knows what is used? Is it a spice, natural, chemical, or ground-up bear glands? Artificial flavors abound. Pets don't need artificial flavors.

- <u>Fructose</u> - Sugar. It should not be used as a flavor enhancer. It can promote the growth of probiotics and beneficial gut bacteria in small amounts.

- <u>Grain fermentation solubles</u> - From particles filtered out during grain fermentation. It adds almost no nutritional value to pet foods.

- <u>Grape pomace</u> - Grape skins, pulp, and seeds. Grapes and raisins are TOXIC to dogs, as is grape-pomace.

- <u>Liver meal</u> - AAFCO defines it a product of ground hepatic glands of mammals. (I never called a liver a gland. I assume they mean gallbladder? That could be called a gland.) It doesn't specify source. It could be from anything from aardvark to zebra. Or 4-D.

- <u>Maltodextrin</u> - This is *Splenda* and *Equal*. It is a sweet carbohydrate with fewer calories than sugar. It is made from wheat, corn, potatoes, or rice so can trigger allergic symptoms. Like any sugar, it is not good for pets.

- <u>Meat and bone meal</u> - The animal parts can be from any source so quality and contamination are unknown. Any kind of animal can be used; goats, pigs, horses, rats, road kill, those euthanized with chemicals, those with maggots (probably a value-added nutrient!), pus, cancer, gangrene, 4-D, etc.

- Oat hulls - Just fiber, comparable to peanut hulls. Has no nutritional value.

- Peanut hulls - Just fiber with no nutritional value. There is the possibility of pesticide residues.

- Poultry byproduct meal - Same as chicken byproduct meal except it can be from any foul. It is from slaughtered animals, not 4-D. There is no control over quality or consistency.

- Poultry fat - This is not specifically from "slaughtered poultry" so can be from any fowl in any condition from any source; buzzards, seagulls, 4-D, geese, road kill, etc.

- Poultry meal - This is not defined as "slaughtered poultry" so can be from any fowl in any condition from any source; buzzards, seagulls, 4-D, geese, road kill, etc.

- Pork and bone meal - Same as beef and bone meal, except made from pork.

- Phosphoric acid - A harmless flavoring used in cola soft drinks, fertilizers, detergents, and pharmaceuticals. Unnecessary in pet foods.

- Potato-product - Peels, culls, rotted parts, etc., of the potato. Quality unknown. Why not use whole potatoes? (Potato-product makes good compost.)

- Propylene glycol - Not harmful in small amount such as used in medicines. It is, however, used as a humectant in soft-moist or semi-moist kibble. Its toxic effects are suspected in animals that daily consume that type of kibble (soft-moist) over a long period of time. It is banned in Europe as a general-purpose food-grade product or direct food additive.

- Rice hulls - Just another source of fiber with no nutritional value.

- Soybean meal - Obtained by grinding the flakes that remain after removal of most of the oil from soybeans by a solvent or mechanical extraction process. It is a poor-quality protein source and has less than 50% of the biologic value of chicken meal.

- Soybean mill run - hulls from the soybean. Commonly referred to as floor sweepings. Filler with little or no nutritional value.

- Sorbitol - Another sugar sweetener completely unnecessary in pet food. Can lead to addiction, overeating, mood swings, tooth decay, arthritis, and allergies.

- Vegetable oil - The product of vegetable origin obtained by extracting the oil from seeds or fruits. The source is unknown; therefore, the nutrient and contaminant properties are unknown. Look for a specific source like corn oil, peanut oil, soybean oil, etc.

- Wheat gluten - It is what makes French bread, pizza dough, and bagels chewy. It can be formed like soy to appear to be meat, duck, or tofu. It is a tough, viscous nitrogenous (protein) substance left after wheat is washed to remove starch. In vegetarian cultures it is widely used. It is a good binder. Depending on the area of the world, gluten is a byproduct of starch production, and in other places the starch is the byproduct of gluten production. The biggest problem with gluten is that it triggers medical problems with many very nonspecific symptoms, usually associated with allergy. Many people don't know they are sensitive to it. Same with pets. It seems best to limit or exclude it from regular diets for that reason.

- Wheat mill run - It is from the "tail of the mill." It is course and fine particles of wheat bran, and fine particles of wheat shorts, wheat germ, wheat flour, and offal. Some refer to it as "floor sweepings." It is inexpensive filler with little or no nutritional value.

- Yeast culture - The dried media on which yeast is grown. Includes some yeast. The media is not identified. Who knows what it actually is? Yeast (a form of mold) will grow on practically anything. Yeast culture can be a flavor enhancer. But it lacks the nutritional value of higher-quality yeast supplements. May contribute to allergies.

- Yeast fermentation solubles - Added as a vitamin B supplement. There are better ways to add vitamin Bs, and the media that the yeast was grown on is not identified.

*The Pet Food Label's *"Nutritional Adequacy Statement"* that claims that a food is complete and balanced is worthless:

The term *"complete and balanced"* is a joke for two reasons:

1. You can create your "complete-and-balanced" pet food by formulating it "to provide levels of nutrients that meet an established profile." This means you never actually have to perform any feeding trials on the product. It just means you borrowed a formula from a Dog Nutrition 101 textbook at

the library and created your dog food to "meet an established profile." "Established-profile"—this term is the quintessence of ambiguous, vague, abstruse, misleading, and indefinite.

2. Or, you can create your "complete-and-balanced" pet food by doing a **"feeding trial protocol."** This is supposedly a better way to prove it is complete and balanced as opposed to "formulated to an established profile." This means that the manufacturer's product, or "lead member of a family of products," has been fed to dogs or cats, under so-called "strict" guidelines, and found to provide complete and balanced nutrition. Well, you say, at least it got fed to some animals and there were "strict" guidelines. It's a joke because here is all they have to do to meet the AAFCO standards of a "feeding trial." Here are the "strict" guidelines:

- 8 dogs make up the test group. (That's a joke right there— only 8?)
- Only 6 are actually required to complete the 26-week trial. (So, 2 could be pulled from the test for any reason and the test could go on.)
- Only the food being tested and water will be available. Duh.
- At the beginning and end the test dogs must pass a physical by a veterinarian. (Whoopee.)
- At the end, but not the beginning, hemoglobin, hematocrit, alkaline phosphatase, and albumen are taken. (There are fifty other blood tests I'd perform.)
- The diet fails if any animal shows signs of nutritional deficiency or excess. Gets too fat? Maybe they ate too much? Loses weight? What exactly are signs that kill the project? Besides, it would be hard for a healthy dog to get noticeably "nutritionally deficient" in six months if fed adequate calories.
- The maximum weight loss is 15%. (That's pretty significant,

actually. I wouldn't want to feed my dog something that would cause him to lose 15% of his weight in six months... unless that was my goal.)

- That's all there is to a so-called "feeding trial." A "strict" feeding trial at that. This completely inadequate protocol is sanctioned by the only oversight there is on the pet food industry, AAFCO, and they have no legal regulatory power anyway.

· 🐕 ·

So, four of us start a dog food company. We call it ***Old Doc & Friends Dog Food.***

We each have two dogs, making eight, so we can do a "feeding trial."

I'm a veterinarian, so I'll examine them day one to make sure they are alive.

We'll feed our concoction for six and a half months, like the rules say. If two of our dogs lose weight or even die, but the other six are okay, so we'll call it a success.

I'll examine them again at the end of the "test" and make sure they are still alive.

When we get our kibble-bags printed we can say we did a *"feeding trial according to AAFCO guidelines."*

We can also print on the bag that it *"tastes like chicken"* because we added 3% chicken—we'll use chicken joint cartilage, chicken lungs, and feet and tails. (Oh, and feathers.)

Ingredients may include peanut hulls from the ballpark, horse manure (a "flavor enhancer"—LOL), corncobs, road kill, apple pumice, newspaper, digest, fish scales, potato peels, shellac, lard, MSG, tartrazine coloring, high-fructose corn syrup, propylene glycol alginate, Carrageenan seaweed, phosphoric acid, bovine growth hormone, gelatin, sodium nitrate, some polysorbate 60, and eyeballs, and sphincters. And bear-glands…why not?

We'll name it:

OLD DOC AND FRIENDS *"Platinum-Quality-Ultra-Premium Natural & Organic Gourmet AAFCO-Approved Complete and Balanced Large and Small Dog Fancy Food with Chicken and Horse Flavor (Free-Range) Human-Grade Energy-Enhanced Working Anti-Shedding Blend with Blueberries, Apple Pomace and Corn Distillers, Dried Grain Run... with Bear."*

Next month we'll come out with *"lamb-flavored-medium-sized-dog"* version.

(Let's begin checking out lamb-bung futures.)

CHAPTER 4

PET FOOD REGULATION AND OVERSIGHT (THERE ISN'T ANY)

This chapter is short because **there is no government agency regulating the pet food industry** to write about. The FDA, USDA, and EPA do not regulate or oversee the pet food industry at all.[13]

---

13 Consumers are protected by **United States Department of Agriculture (USDA)** programs that regulate and monitor soil, water, and wildlife on privately owned property; rural drinking water; and meat, poultry, and egg products. They are charged with ensuring **people** a safe, affordable, nutritious, and accessible food supply. They administer a variety of food-related programs, all of which either assist suppliers or protect consumers. **The USDA does not regulate pet food.**
The **Food and Drug Administration (FDA)** is part of the U.S. Department of Health and human Services (DHHS). The FDA provides oversight of food, drugs, and related products. They protect public health by ensuring the safety of the production, processing, and packaging, storing, and holding of all domestic and imported foods, except for those products that are under the jurisdiction of the U.S. Department of Agriculture. They also are responsible for safeguarding all ingredients used in human food products, approving new food additives, monitoring ingredients and foods to see that they are contaminant free, and monitoring dietary supplements, infant formulas, and medical foods for safety. The FDA oversees human food labeling and requires that food product labels be informative, truthful, and useful to the consumer. **The FDA does not oversee the pet food industry.**
The World Health Organization **(WHO)** assures the safety of the world food supply through its Food Safety Department, resulting in the reduction of the negative impact of food-borne disease worldwide. **They do not oversee the pet food industry.**
The Environmental Protection Agency **(EPA)** regulates pesticides usage and the establishment of water quality standards for the United States. The Centers for Disease Control and Prevention **(CDC)** have a Food Safety Initiative Activity that focuses solely on the prevention of food-borne illness. **The EPA does not oversee the pet food industry.** So, the USDA, FDA, CDC, and EPA all regulate things going into pet food at some level, but not the manufacture of the pet food itself.

There is only one organization "watching" the pet food industry (sort of). The AAFCO (*Association of American Feed Control Officials*) sets guidelines and definitions for animal feed, including pet foods. AAFCO is a volunteer nonprofit organization made up of local, state, and federal officials, and pet food industry specialists (many that work in the pet food industry), and educators. It sets standards for quality and safety of animal feed and pet food in the U.S.

According to the AAFCO website, it "provides a forum for the membership and industry representation to achieve three main goals."

- Ensure consumer protection.
- Safeguard the health of animals and humans.
- Provide a level playing field of orderly commerce for the animal feed industry.

It has zero regulatory legal authority. It is not a government agency. There are government officials serving on AAFCO that may already be involved in the enforcement of laws and regulations concerning the safety of animal feed (they may work for the USDA, FDA, EPA, etc.). So, while performing their government job they may be involved at some level in regulation and safety considerations of the raw ingredients the pet food industry may obtain for their pet foods, but they don't regulate how those ingredients are used in pet food manufacture. That is solely up to the pet food manufacturers. And as discovered in 2007 (melamine disaster), if AAFCO was "watching" then, they dropped the ball.[14]

The truth is, AAFCO doesn't do much, but that's all we've got.

There is one attempt to help prevent another disaster like the melamine poisoning. The FDA has established a program called *The Partnership for Food Protection* within its organization.

---

14 There are inspectors employed at many levels of the food chain, but mostly for the human food supply, not its byproducts. It is at best a hit-and-miss proposition. Every tank car, boxcar, shipping container, refrigerator car, hopper, silo, etc., cannot be inspected. Most rendering operations aren't inspected at all. It's like building code inspectors—impossible to cover everything at all times—so stadium roofs cave in under heavy snow.

The purpose is to bring federal, state, local, territorial, and tribal representatives with expertise in food, feed, epidemiology, laboratory, animal health, and environmental and public health, together to develop and Integrated Food Safety System. One of its programs is the **Pet Event Tracking Network (PETNet).**

PETNet is a secure, web-based information exchange system that will allow the FDA and federal and state agencies to share information about pet food-related incidents, such as an illness associated with the consumption of pet food or pet food product defects.

Members will enter "events" into the system when they have identified a trend or a suspicious incident associated with pet food products, and that information will be immediately available to all other PETNet members for collaboration.

Hopefully this system of communication will minimize another poisoning. However, it won't kick in until some disaster has already started and pets are sick, dying, or dead already. It isn't going to prevent much, if anything. It may cut some losses.

Again, your pet is part of your pet food manufacture's long-range feeding trials. Who knows what's really in that bag of dog food? Who knows what the daily feeding of that food will cause during your pet's lifespan? At least with PETNet up and running we may be able to stop a mass poisoning from factory manufactured pet foods while the disastrous effects are small. (But the suffering of even one pet is intolerable.)

So much for pet food regulation and oversight; not much to it, is there?

CHAPTER 5

THE SCIENCE OF NUTRITION

You can skip this chapter completely. There won't be a test on it Monday. Remember, you don't have to be a scientist to feed your dog. It's an interesting chapter, though!

Eskimos eat blubber. Italians eat pasta. Kansans eat beef. Iowans eat corn. Irish eat potatoes. Chinese eat rice. Dogs eat anything. Cats would love a couple of parakeets and a hamster every day. The point is that our bodies can use nearly anything for energy/nutrition at the metabolic/chemical/molecular level. That's the bedrock belief of the pet food industry, and they are right.

After food is put in a mouth, it's smashed, macerated, pulverized, swallowed, boiled in stomach acid, assaulted by intestinal enzymes, liquefied, fermented, squeezed, squirted, shaken, mixed, blended, and absorbed into the bloodstream. No matter what it was in the beginning, it is becomes a bunch of molecules that bear no resemblance to the tossed salad with ranch dressing and bacon bits, steak, baked potato, butter, sour cream, wine, coffee, and chocolate mousse that it started out as.

Protein, carbohydrates, and fat is what it all boils down to after your stomach and intestines have done their job. These molecules become lots of things: energy, muscle, brain cells, red blood cells, DNA, a cell wall, a toenail, maybe a uterus, a new life, and then finally trash, which is further dried, formed, compressed, fermented…and sent out the garbage chute.

Steak and potato and blubber and rice and pasta end up becoming adenosine tri-phosphate, pyruvate dehydrogenase, succinyl-CoA synthetase, isocitrate, fumarase, a-ketoglutarate dehydrogenase, aconitase, malate dehydrogenase…then end up in processes called glycolysis and the Szent-Gyorgyi-Krebs cycle…whatever…yawn. There is a lot going on with oxygen and water too!

A margarita can become a lip. A taco can become tooth enamel. Chocolate cake a tear. Ice cream…well, it's headed to a life sentence in a "fat cell" at Adipose Prison.

Our food replaces 98% of the atoms in our body a year. The skeleton turns over every three months. Skin is new once a month. Intestinal lining cells in the small intestine are replaced every 72 hours, and in the large intestine, every 12 days. Everything we eat becomes a processed byproduct and routed to where it needs to go. Scientific formulation of pet food is based on this. The body doesn't know the difference between whole food and byproducts if everything is mixed right.

The really big picture: Everything comes from the sun— everything is the result of the sun's delivered energy to the planet. We either eat the plants the sun grows, or we eat what eats the plants. Energy from the sun is stored in the plant in high-energy phosphate compounds like adenosine triphosphate, or ATP. ATP is the "fuel" of the body. ATP pumps ions, drives molecular construction, and activates contractile muscle proteins. It fuels the furnace to make heat. A molecule of glucose will make 30 or 40 ATPs. There is about eight pounds of ATP in your body. It recycles itself, leaving carbon dioxide and water, and some ammonia. That is life. The big picture—it all comes from the sun one way or another. Food is just stored sun energy, no matter what kind of food it is.

Whatever food you or your pet swallow, the stored energy in it will be used by the body to make tissue, or for energy. Almost everything your body needs it can synthesize on its own using a balanced food source for the necessary building blocks. But there are some things your body can't make for itself. These include minerals, some specific amino acids (amino acids are the "building blocks" for protein manufacture), some vitamins (which are really catalysts, which alter the rate of a chemical reaction), some essential (you can't make them yourself) fatty acids, and so on. The lack of these will result in a "deficiency."

Also, important: There has to be the proper ratios of certain things in our diet that are the same ratios of those same things in our body. For instance, you, and your pets' bodies, require a ratio of two calcium molecules for every one phosphorous molecule. In fact, our bones are made of di-calcium phosphate, which is two calcium and one phosphorous. So, if we have a diet with high phosphorous and low calcium, we will be "deficient" in calcium. This is, in fact, what happens if all we eat is meat. Skeletal muscle (meat) is very low in calcium. So, we eat dairy products (rich in calcium) to offset that deficiency. A calcium deficiency will eventually cause a robbing of the calcium from the bones to keep the calcium level up in the blood, because the heart will literally stop beating if there is not adequate calcium in the blood. The bones that donate calcium will become so decalcified that they will turn into the consistency of rubber, and even break spontaneously.

Another example of a proper-ratio-problem concerns the "essential" (we can't make them) fatty acids. Omega-3 and omega-6 essential fatty acids should be at a 1:1 ratio. Omega-6 is sort of **bad**...while omega-3 is sort of **good**. Vegetable oils (from grain, which is used heavily in pet foods because it is cheap) can have as much as **30 times** as much omega-6 as omega-3[15]. Not good. Fish oils (salmon, mackerel, herring), and animal sources

---

15 See the chapter on Supplements for an in-depth discussion on these fatty acids.

such as meat and egg yolks, are rich in omega-3 essential fatty acids and can offset the imbalance seen in most pet foods that rely heavily on grain ingredients.

Pretty much every kibble-style pet food is deficient in omega-3s. This is why veterinarians recommend supplementing your pet's diet with fish oils, and other sources of omega-3 essential fatty acids. The health of the skin is commonly a "sentinel" or "canary-in-the-mine" for showing the need to increase omega-3s in a pet's diet. (Dry, dull, flaky, itchy hair coat = low omega-3s.)

Over the last 150 years the human intake of omega-6 has increased…and the intake of omega-3 has decreased. This has resulted in the increase in heart disease. This is why we are encouraged to take "cold-water" fish oil supplements as those fish have high levels of omega-3 fatty acids.

Blood tests rarely detect nutritional imbalances. This is because the body maintains homeostasis in the blood by robbing Peter to pay Paul. For example, the body keeps the blood calcium/phosphorous ratio 2 to 1 no matter what the cost is to another part of the body, such as the skeletal system, or the heart will quit working.

The identification and correction of deficiencies and imbalances is exactly what happened in the early years (just post-WWII) of commercial pet food manufacture. Calcium deficiency was common then largely because horse meat was a very common ingredient in cans for pets. (With the mechanization of farming, horses were a surplus.) Muscle (horse) meat is low in calcium. Pets' bones began spontaneously breaking due to the lack of calcium. Scientists (pet food scientists) added crushed oyster shell dusted on top of canned all-meat diets to offset this calcium deficiency. Oyster shells are made of calcium carbonate, or basically pure calcium. This brought the ratio back to the normal 2:1 calcium to phosphorous. (Crushed oyster shells compressed into tablets are a still a common source of calcium supplementation for women to prevent osteoporosis due to a calcium deficiency.)

Often people choose vegetarian diets for themselves due to

ethical concerns—and sometimes their pets too. <u>But cats are</u> **<u>obligate carnivores</u>** <u>and vegetarian diets cannot meet feline</u> <u>requirements, period.</u> The long-term nutritional adequacy of vegetarian diets in dogs is unclear, but one survey study of vegetarian diets in dogs in Europe showed that nutritional problems were nearly universal with these diets. Supplementing at least with eggs, and dairy products, is absolutely necessary for "vegan" dogs.

So, no matter what we, and our pets eat, our bodies break it down into molecular-sized biochemical metabolites, which end up where they are needed, or are stored for later use. There are some potential deficiencies and balances to look out for. <u>This</u> <u>deficiency-and-balance issue is</u> **<u>THE</u>** <u>pet food manufactures'</u> **<u>ENTIRE PREMIS</u>** <u>of why you are too</u> **<u>dumb</u>** <u>to feed your pets.</u> They are taking the position that only they are smart enough to prevent these deficiencies and prevent imbalances in your pet's diet, so therefore if you are making pet food, you are going to screw up your pet. This is nonsense. But they have been taking that stand for well over a half a century—to the point of actually making it a universally accepted "truth" (even for graduating veterinary students!).

However, a growing number of pet owners, veterinarians, and other pet professionals have come to the conclusion that this is no longer the case. In fact, rather than trust the pet food manufactures' science (witness: the melamine/cyanuric acid disaster, and the recent cardiomyopathy incident increase), we actually believe that the pet food manufactures may be doing *harm to our pets*. We believe **wholesomeness** is just as important as being balanced and complete.

So, I ask, why not just use "whole" foods instead of trying to balance parts of foods?

So much for the science; let's start cooking whole foods.

THE CANINE FOOD PYRAMID

CHAPTER 6

COOKING FOR YOUR DOG

The overall theme of cooking for your pet is the use of "whole" ingredients, instead of fractions and fragments of food. For instance, there are over 500 nutrients in a whole carrot (only ten of which end up in multiple vitamins). Beta-carotene is just a small part of a carrot's many nutrients. Each step of extracting nutrients from a whole food leaves fractions of the whole. Then, a scientist combines these fractions, and fragments, back into something resembling a balanced and complete whole (Frankenfood). This is the basis for commercial pet food manufacturing (it takes a scientist). At home, your pet food manufacturing uses only whole foods. They are balanced and complete already.

"Whole foods" are **defined** as: *foods in their original form; grown in fertile soil and harvested without refinement; and containing a complex array of essential nutrients, enzymes, phytochemicals,*[16] *and anti-oxidants to support health.* (The way they come off the tree, vine, field, or hoof.)

A "matrix" in food amplifies and synergizes each ingredient.

---

16 Phytochemical compounds in plants act as antimicrobials, antifungals, and insecticides to combat bacteria, molds, insects, bad weather, etc.

Isolate one ingredient and it acts differently by itself than when still in the whole food form that it came from. Synthesize something found in whole food, and it acts differently than the real thing. *Food synergy* is defined as the added health benefits that food and their parts contribute as a whole. This means that the benefits from any food constituent by itself may not be the equivalent of what its value is as when it is included with other whole foods.

You can call this "holistic," if you want. Or just common sense. Or, how about rounded, complete, all-inclusive, full, or whole?

Vitamins exist in a complex form. There is no such thing as a vitamin B1 tree or an ascorbic acid (vitamin C) orange. Vitamins always exist in a complex form with co-vitamins, trace-minerals, unknown substances, enzymes, etc. The extracts, or those artificially compounded, lack all these things. Our bodies are complex, and so should be our food.

There is also synergy[17] between foods. For instance, in one study, fish and broccoli in combination was 13 times more effective in the reduction of lipid oxidation than either food alone.[18] In another study an orange/apple/grape/blueberry combination showed 5 times the antioxidant activity of any one fruit or berry fed alone.[19] Marjoram added to salad greens increased the antioxidant capacity by 200%.[20] Curry, and olive oil, act in synergy in recipes from India. Our cultures have embraced these synergies in their recipes and cooking styles for millennia.

In a classic Japanese study laboratory rats were given dimethyl-benzanthracene (DMBA) daily, which caused a 100% breast tumor formation. Different groups on DMBA were given different combinations of supplements to see if supplementation would

---

17 Synergy: The simultaneous action of separate agencies which, together, have a greater total effect than the sum of their individual affects.

18 Judith DeCava, 2006, *Good Foods, Bad Foods, and the Real Truth About Vitamins and Antioxidants.*

19 Liu, 2004.

20 Ninfali, 2005.

decrease the DMBA's cancer-causing effect:[21] The supplements included were:
- Selenium (from cereals, vegetables, fish, shellfish).
- Magnesium (from spinach, almonds, hazelnuts, whole-grain cereals).
- Vitamin C (from fruits, vegetables, cabbage, strawberries).
- Vitamin A (from bright-colored fruits and vegetables, eggs).

Tumor incidence was dramatically reduced when given those supple- ments in combination (synergy).

1. No supplement...100% incidence of cancer, as expected.
2. Feeding just one substance (from the list above) reduced the incidence of cancer by 50%.
3. Feeding two supplements...a 76% decrease in the incidence of cancer.
4. Feeding three supplements...an 80% decrease.
5. Feeding all four...an 88% decrease.

Remove one component of a watch and it fails to function.

Also:

Fractions of food cause allergic reactions more so than the whole food it came from. A pet is more likely to develop allergy reactions to wheat byproducts, beef byproducts, generic fats, synthetic preservatives, antibiotic residue, etc., than whole foods.

On a side note: An advantage of home cooking for allergy dogs is that you can exclude a certain ingredient easily. This is impossible using commercial pet foods because there is so much other stuff in the bag that can contribute to the allergic response, including dyes, preservatives, toxins, etc. Try feeding your allergy pet just one ingredient at a time, adding one more as you go along,

---

21 Ramesha, A. N., et al, "Chemoprevention of 7,12-Dimethylbenzanthracene-Induced Mammary Carcinogenesis in Rat by the combined actions of Se, Mg, Ascorbic Acid, and Retinyl Acetate," *Japanese Journal of Cancer Research* 81, no. 12 (1990): 1239-46.

until you see symptoms. (This is one-way veterinarians diagnose food allergy.)[22]

• 🐾 •

Home cooking for your dog...a recipe to start with:
(This is so simple, even a caveman can do it. Wait a minute... cavemen did do it!)

Recipe ONE

I call it "Under the ground—on the ground—above the ground—eggs—meat—dairy."

1. Into a large stew pot slice and dice carrots, potatoes, and sweet potatoes (vegetables that come from **UNDER** the ground).
2. Add a bag of frozen mixed vegetables (grown **ON** the ground).
3. Grain: Add rice, pasta, and oatmeal, on top of the previous two layers (grain grows **ABOVE** the ground).
4. Add broth (flavor enhancer) or water, sufficient quantity to cook the grains—usually twice the volume of the grains. (For instance, to cook one pound of rice it takes two pounds of liquid. Since a pint contains 16 ounces (it weighs a pound), for one pound of grain add two pints, or 32 ounces, or 4 cups (one cup = 8 oz). Remember the ditty: "A pound...a pint...two cups."
5. Then add a dozen eggs scrambled.
6. Add a pound of shredded cheese—real dairy cheese.
7. Finally, add a two-to-three-inch-thick layer of hamburger (80:20) on top. Add a little iodized salt. Cover and bake in the oven on 275-325°F until meat is done (split the hamburger open occasionally to check until it is at least pink). The

---

22 Food allergy symptoms in dogs and cats can start when they are under a year of age. They actually get the sensitivity to foods while in the womb. In order to become sensitized to other stuff the world has to offer, they have to be alive for a while. Itchy feet, itchy ears, and itchy rears in young animals under a year of age are often food allergy related. It makes sense to cook for these dogs to try to exclude what they are sensitive to.

concoction does not have to be well done—a little pinkness in the meat and crunch in the veggies is not a bad thing.

8. Serve with cottage cheese.

The meat drippings/fat are soaked up by the ingredients as they cook. The broth infuses the vegetables and grains with flavor.

Just scoop out a portion with all the layers, like serving lasagna. Freeze extra.

Recipe TWO

This uses chicken or turkey (whole chickens, thighs, halves, ribs and breast, turkey breast, or boneless thighs, etc.).

1. Boil or bake the chicken in some lightly salted (iodized) water with some carrots, potatoes, and sweet potatoes. (You'll cut it all up later, after it's cooked and cooled.)
2. Take out the chicken and vegetables when they are done. Skim the fat if there is a lot (unless your dog is running the Iditarod in minus-thirty-degree weather—he'll need the energy from extra fat.)
3. In the soup you just made put in a pound of rice, a bag of egg noodles or macaroni (or any kind of pasta), a cup or two of oatmeal, a cup of cornmeal… and cook until the grains are done. Add water or chicken/beef/vegetable broth if more liquid is needed. Remember, it takes about twice the volume of liquid than the grains to cook the grains. Too much liquid is not a bad thing—extra fluid is good.
4. Then add a dozen scrambled eggs and stir them in. Cook some more.
5. Meanwhile, debone the chicken/turkey.
6. Put the meat back in with the cooked grains, vegetables, and eggs. Cook a little more until the "casserole" is pasty. Mix in some unsweetened yogurt, cottage cheese, or leftover cheese for the calcium and added animal-sourced protein. Quality

leftovers such as hotdogs, meatloaf, cooked hamburgers, etc., can be added too.

7. Let cool, and serve with some cottage cheese. Your dog will go absolutely ape.

Freeze the rest and thaw portions when you need it. My dogs eat this cold out of the refrigerator, or slightly warmed in the microwave—they really don't care.

Keep some high-quality dry (stay away from soft-moist[23]) dog food out to fill them up if they don't get enough of your food. Good-quality whole-food-style commercially prepared foods can also fill in possible nutritional gaps in your homecooked food. **You want commercial dog food to supplement your food, not your food supplementing commercial food**.

That's it. All you need to know. All you need to read. You can stop reading and start cooking.

Amount? Their stomachs are huge. They will eat all you give them but they don't need more than a cup per 10 or twenty pounds. Breeds, age, and levels of activity cause animals to vary individually in the amount of food needed. Home cooking seems to satisfy and satiate them so they tend not to overeat. Their energy is even, as opposed to the highs and lows of a high-carbohydrate diet. They only need fed your food once a day. Food stays in their stomach a lot longer than food stays in our stomachs. But you can feed them ten times a day if you want.

Home-cooked food has higher water content than dry food, so they need more of it than dry. This high-moisture food is great for all pets. Dry kibble can irritate the stomach and will sap water from other body systems, causing a temporary dehydration (particularly in cats). Try eating a bag of popcorn without a beverage. Eating

---

23 Propylene glycol is used as a humectant to keep soft-moist/semi-moist kibble from drying out. It can be ingested in small amounts. Many drugs use it as a solvent to liquefy or dilute the actual drug. But it may be toxic if consumed in large amounts daily for months at a time, such as the case in soft moist pet food. In Europe it is not cleared as a general- purpose food-grade product or additive.

dry kibble to a stomach is like eating a "Cup-of-Soup" without adding the water.

Pets can have portions of what you eat too throughout the day. Don't give them the fat and gristle; give them the good stuff like you eat. Watch the sugar and spices.

Recipe THREE

1. Make a meatloaf. Hamburger or turkey burger. A little iodized salt.
2. Mix in precooked rice/pasta/oatmeal/grits, or breadcrumbs, etc.
3. Add potatoes, carrots, mixed vegetables, eggs, cheese, and bake as you would any meatloaf, around 275 to 325°F.
4. Slice into meal-sized portions and freeze.

Note: I use any inexpensive/on sale poultry and meat I can find, including turkey, fish, pork, and even things like liver, kidney, tongue, etc. Bake it or boil it. Or cook it in a Crockpot.

MY PERSONAL RECIPE

I fill a large oval turkey cooker with every kind of food I can find and cook it overnight at 225°F. Nothing burns at that temp. (Try cooking a brisket that way—works like a charm—a (fat removed) brisket, a bottle of your favorite BB sauce, and cook slowly over night.)

I start with ten pounds of hamburger (not lean—fat is good in this case), a pound each of rice, oatmeal, and pasta (wheat) of any kind, a couple pounds of mixed vegetables (canned or frozen), a pound of beans (any kind), two dozen eggs scrambled, a couple pounds of shredded cheese (real cheese), minced potatoes (including sweet), and a gallon of beef broth.

Or I use chicken. And chicken broth. I buy chicken thighs or whole chickens and pick the bones out after cooking. Interestingly, chickens for consumption are very young and the bones are not well calcified. Cooking them overnight makes the bones soft and not dangerous like bones from fried chicken. Those bones are digestible in most cases…so if you miss a few, it's no big deal if the chicken has been cooked slow overnight.

I will add leftover bread, bacon and sausage, livers, necks, hearts, gizzards, whole carrots (dogs love cooked carrots in broth), kidneys… really anything that is cheap and often unwanted for the human dinner table.

It doesn't have to be well mixed any more than food has to be mixed on your plate. The stomach will do it for you. Or one meal may contain more of one ingredient today, and more of another tomorrow. Every meal does not have to be "balanced."

OTHER FOODS YOU CAN FEED YOUR PET

Olive oil, fish oil, sprouts, squash, cabbage, bok choy, wheat germ, wheat flower, any kind of pasta, shrimp, parsley, apple, cherries, peaches (fruit less the seeds—seeds may contain cyanides), banana, kale, carrots, corn, collard greens, celery, cream of mushroom or celery soup, mashed potatoes, baked potatoes, sweet potatoes, French fries, cream of wheat, parsnips, butter, hardboiled eggs, kelp, yeast, peanut butter, bagel, English muffin, rye bread, pita, tortilla, bran flakes, shredded wheat, Chex, tapioca, popcorn, beans (lima, white, red, black, soy, pinto, kidney, etc.), canned pumpkin (good laxative), rabbit, deer, squirrel, pheasant, mackerel, clams, crab, lobster, oysters, scallops, luncheon meats, cheese spreads, hotdogs, cream, cream cheese, sour cream, peas, string beans, chickpeas, broccoli, Brussels sprouts, cauliflower, spinach, watercress, asparagus, cucumber, lettuce, zucchini, eggplant, mushrooms, green peppers, tomatoes, cranberries, blueberries, strawberries, raspberries, liver, kidney, heart, tongue, tripe, chicken necks and backs—all are safe and nutritious.

You can give your dog peanut butter (no xylitol) sandwiches without the jelly or jam as a treat.

Out of your homemade food? Cook up a frozen pot pie. Or a can of hash with an egg. "Balancing" your pet's food is not any more difficult than feeding your family. Variety is the key.

Treats: Commercial treats are just more of the same junk—just high-priced dog food. In fact, they are usually worse than commercial dog food because they are full of taste-tempting fat. Forget them.

Instead, give them parboiled vegetables, hardboiled egg, string cheese, peanut butter and crackers, meatballs, vegetables soaked in broth, raw carrot, a hunk of cooked lasagna noodle, a blueberry, a piece of banana or apple, lima beans soaked in broth, multigrain bread, last night's hamburger or meatloaf, and yes, bones.

Bones are universally adored by all dogs. Dogs and bones go way back. Nothing can bliss out a dog like chewing a bone. They are very oral creatures. But they are really stupid about what they swallow. The thing is…you're darned if you do, and darned if you don't. If you don't give them a bone, they'll find something else to chew.

So, you have to be smart about giving dogs bones. They have big mouths—they seem to be able to swallow anything, like a python. They have strong teeth and jaws. In fact, they bite with 4000 pounds of pressure per square inch, as opposed to our puny 400 pounds per square inch. So, they sometimes break their teeth. Or they break off chunks of the bone and swallow them. You have to try to find a bone big enough that they can't break it up. (Of course, when you give the little dog an appropriate bone, the big dog will find it and swallow it.)

It has been rare in my 40-plus years as a vet that I have had to take a bone out of a dog surgically. I can't even remember the last time. I've had bones get stuck in the roof of their mouth between their upper molars. And around their lower jaw. I have had bones wedged sideways in their colon. I've done lots of enemas for bones (and pantyhose, underwear, socks, rocks, wood chips, squeaky toys, rawhide, TV remotes, you name it). But bones don't cause that many problems if you are careful.

Guidelines:
1. Bigger than they can swallow.
2. Trim it but leave some fat, ligaments, and the marrow.
3. Boil it a little in broth, or bake for a half an hour. Cook a bunch at the same time and freeze them. You can pass them

out frozen—dogs don't care. Cooking awakens the flavor and sterilizes them.

4. Recycle them. After a day, re-boil them in broth, and give them again.
5. Throw them away before they get rancid.
6. Cooked chicken bones and pork bones should be avoided. Interestingly raw chicken bones are well tolerated by large dogs.

SUBSTANCES TOXIC TO PETS
Animal Poison Control Center hotline 24/7: **1-800-222-1222,**
or **triage.webpoisoncontrol.org**

- Avocado: The toxic parts are the wood, bark, leaves, pit, and skin of the avocado; can cause fluid accumulation in the lungs and abdomen, making breathing difficult. The toxic principle in avocado is a fungicidal toxin called "persin." It can leach into the meat of the avocado from the pits. Persin is toxic to dogs but not humans.

- Macadamia nuts and walnuts: Researchers are not sure why these can be toxic but they can cause vomiting, lameness, tremors, depression, and stiffness.

- Onions and garlic: These contain thiosulphate and when consumed regularly or in large amounts may cause a dog's red blood cells to weaken (exhibiting denatured hemoglobin called Heinz bodies). These damaged red blood cells break apart and lead to anemia. We humans have an enzyme that allows us to digest onions and garlic. Note: Garlic can be a powerful appetite enhancer for dogs. They can handle a little. Add a little powder as a flavor enhancer.

- Grapes and raisins: These cause kidney failure in dogs for an unclear reason. This includes wine, and any product made from grapes, or a supplement containing grapes, or grape seed/ leaves extract (which has become popular in human nutrition, supposedly helping with high cholesterol, eye diseases, diabetes, etc.).

- Nutmeg: Can cause central nervous system problems including tremors, seizures, etc.

- Alcohol: Some dogs can be attracted to certain mixed drinks and beer. Alcohol toxicity is dangerous in dogs, causing all the signs seen in humans, only worse, and quicker. It can be fatal.

- Yeast dough (unbaked bread): After a dog consumes dough it continues to rise in their stomach, causing distention and pain, as well as possible alcohol poisoning from the yeast fermenting.

- Caffeine and chocolate: **Caffeine,** and **theobromine** found in chocolate, act as a nervous system stimulant. They can cause restlessness, hyperactivity, muscle twitching, increased urination, seizures, increased heart rate, and increased blood pressure. Don't let a dog get into the trash and eat coffee grounds. An M&M is milk chocolate and low in the dark chocolate that causes the problem. A dropped piece of candy isn't going to kill your dog. In fact, I have had dogs eat an entire pound of milk chocolates (including the box they came in) with no effect other than diarrhea.

  Milk chocolate: has 64 mgs of theobromine and caffeine per ounce.
  Dark chocolate: 150 mgs
  Baker's chocolate: 450 mgs
  Cocoa powder: 800 mgs

- Xylitol sweetener: a popular sugar substitute that is highly toxic to dogs. It is used in chewing gum extensively. Now in peanut butter too. And recently in *Pepto Bismol.* A few pieces of xylitol-containing gum within 30 minutes can cause vomiting, lethargy, loss of coordination, possible collapse, and possible seizure. The dog's blood sugar level drops dramatically. There is often liver failure within a day. We are not sure why dogs react to Xylitol.

- Tylenol, Advil, and Ibuprofen: These are highly toxic to dogs and cats because they cannot metabolize them, so they accumulate to toxic levels. Only aspirin and prescription veterinary painkillers are safe for dogs. Cats shouldn't take aspirin.

If you do an internet search for homemade pet diets, you'll get 8.9 million hits. But you don't really need to collect recipes. Just make your pets meals out of whole foods and use a lot of variety. Don't make it any more complicated than it has to be. Don't get scientific—you don't need to.

Use a high-quality commercial dog food as a supplement, not your food to supplement commercial food.

One final thing: I can't count how many dog owners mention that since they started cooking for their dog, their dog's breath will no longer stop a train, or peel paint.

offthemark.com

Permission for Williams to use cartoon in print/electronic.

CHAPTER 7

COOKING FOR YOUR CAT

Sylvester and Tweety...that relationship goes way back! The perfect diet for a cat: four parakeets a day.

Cats are carnivores. Not **CORN**-ivores. **THEY EAT MEAT**. Cats are highly evolved predators who have hunted and eaten rodents, birds, snakes, frogs, and other small creatures for thousands of years. They are very heavy into protein in their diet—not carbohydrates. Why are we feeding them corn? (Most commercial dry cat foods use corn.)

Pet food labels are not required to have the percentage of carbs in the food. Add all the other percentages (protein, fat, fiber, moisture), subtract that from 100%, you can sort of figure out the carb content percentage. Why not give the percentage of carbs on the label? Who knows? (Normal pet-food-industry-slight-of-hand?)

Carbohydrates are sugars and starches. Cats cannot digest sugars (sucrose) at all. They can digest small amounts of cooked starches, like found in Cassava flour, rice, corn, sorghum, pea, lentil. So, yes, starches can be digested, but cats have only small amounts of enzymes to digest starch, so starches are only absorbed if they eat small amounts 4-8 times a day...which the pet food industry hopes that your cat will do; it is typical that a cat "grazes," as opposed to "wolfing" food like a dog. Okay, fine, they CAN digest carbs...sort of...ish. But not a lot at once. Why bother? Why not just feed meat? Oh—corn is cheap. Yes, CORN IS CHEAP!

Here's some science about cats.[24] (If you have a cat you really need to read this—there WILL be a test Monday.):

- They are **obligatory carnivores**. This means they have to have protein in their diet. They use protein for energy, even if there is a large amount of carbohydrates to use. Other species, including dogs, are able to use carbohydrates. But not cats.
- The cat can only use protein to make energy. Most other animals, including humans, only burn protein for energy when protein is plentiful in their diet. We can use carbohydrates for energy. Cats cannot. Cats cannot shut off their protein burner. They need a high-protein, low-carbohydrate diet.
- Proteins are made from amino acids. There are some amino acids essential to a cat's existence that can only be found in animal protein (taurine, arginine, methionine, and cysteine). Corn-based cat foods have to add these. (It takes a scientist.)
- Cats cannot convert the essential fatty acid called linoleic acid to arachidonic acid like most other mammals. Arachidonic acid is not found in plants. Arachidonic acid is essential for the membranes of brain, muscle, and liver cells. Cats have to have animal protein in their diet to get this essential fatty acid.
- Cats require vitamin A and D from animal sources to be present in their "active" form because they are unable to synthesize them in their skin using plant precursors and sunlight.
- Cats need certain B vitamins in their diet in higher amounts than most other mammals (thiamin, pyridoxine, niacin, pantothenic acid).

---

24 Ref: Debra Zoran, DVM, Ph.D., DACVIM, Texas A&M University, College Station, TX, "What Should I Feed That Cat?" notes from 2010 Missouri State Veterinary Conference.

- Cats have no amylase in their saliva. Amylase is an enzyme that helps digest carbohydrates. They also have reduced amylase in the intestine. Amylase is made by the pancreas and squirted into the small intestine as needed to digest carbs, so their efficiency in digesting carbohydrates is limited, as pointed out before.
- The small intestine of cats is much shorter proportionally than omnivores. Longer intestines are necessary for digesting complex carbohydrates.
- Cats have only 30 permanent teeth while dogs have 42. The cat's jaw has far less mobility from side to side than a dog. This means they are not built for grinding vegetable material (kibble) at all.
- *This one is important:* Cats have insufficient liver enzymes to convert glucose to glycogen and so after eating they cannot deal with the sugar load caused by high carbs in the food. Dogs and humans can. Additionally, cats have no enzymes to utilize other sugars like fructose.
- All this is why so many cats suffer from obesity and diabetes.

Whoever heard of vegetarian mountain lions? In the wild, felines consume very little plant material (except what is in the intestinal tract of their prey). Carbohydrates normally amount to only 5% or so of their total dietary intake. But commercial cat foods have 30 to 70% carbohydrates in them! That's definitely hard to believe. One reason is that dry cat food kibble actually cannot be made using industrial extruders without a lot of carbohydrates to hold the kibble together.

Kibble is not good for your cat. Period.

Some pet food companies now substitute with potato—which is a starch—to hold kibble together instead of grain, and then call it "grain-free." Hmm? This is why "grain-free" pet foods (for dogs and cats) are maybe even worse than those with grain. It's just a marketing tool, as humans are into "grain-free." (For the fad-anti-gluten crowd.)

This high level of carbs in our domestic cats' diet wreaks havoc. The problems resulting from high-carb feline diets include obesity, diabetes, hepatic lipidosis, inflammatory bowel disease, juvenile feline diarrhea, and feline dental resorptive disease. It is also thought to be implicated in chronic renal disease in cats, feline urinary syndrome, constipation, and all sorts of allergy problems. And chronic vomiting.

Some say that cats are just vomit-varmints—that's what they do! Not really…it's often just the dry food they have eaten whole that is seriously irritating their stomachs. (Try eating a *Cup-of-Soup*, or *Ramen,* without the water.) Many cats vomit dry kibble up because the stomach just isn't buying it. We give hairballs too much credit.

Cats have a unique system that tells them to stop eating. If they eat food rich in protein and fat, a signal tells them they have had enough calories, so they quit eating. Not so with carbohydrates in cat food. A high-carb diet in cats has a minimal effect on satiation, even if the cat has met its energy requirements, or exceeded it. This is an idiosyncrasy unique to cats. Dry high-carb cat foods cannot satisfy them—or make them feel full. "They always seem to be hungry." Or owners think the cat loves the food so much that it must be good… that's why they overeat. But, it's really because they cannot feel satiated.

Neutering and spaying also contribute to obesity, as does their indoor sedentary lifestyle. Pair this with a high-carbohydrate diet, and you have a "perfect storm."

Pet food companies often list a meat source as first on their label, indicating that meat makes up the largest percentage of the formula. But…this is usually followed by three or four grains that, when added together, make up a much higher percentage of the food than the meat.

Even more than dogs, cats have been gravely affected by commercial foods.

Short of raising mice and parakeets, what can we do? No longer able to hunt, or even recognizing prey as food (most would just play with the mouse for a while, then waddle to food bowl), they will probably not eat a rodent, or bird, anyway. They literally become addicted to carbs like a child to sugar. Additionally, they are quintessential creatures of habit. Dogs will try anything. Cats would rather not eat than try something new. Dogs are rowdy, in-your-face beggars, shameless, take-a-chance, anything goes. Cats are standoffish, reclusive, quiet, solitary, and not trusting. Getting them to eat right, after years of habitual grazing of dry food, can be daunting (and maybe even impossible).

Adding to the "perfect storm" in cat food nutrition is the fact that they are essentially desert animals (think Egypt). They are not good water drinkers. They can concentrate their urine (hence, conserve body fluids) many times what humans can do. (That's why their urine often smells so strong.) In fact, some specialists in veterinary nutrition say if you see a cat drinking, something is wrong.

But you can't just add water to dry cat food to make it okay.

DRY cat foods have 25 to 50 percent dry carbohydrates, 20 to 30 percent dry proteins, and 10 to 25 percent dry fat. This is as much as 25 times the carbohydrates found in **canned** food! And as we now know...cats can't digest carbs...so are you kidding me? Really?! What are these pet food companies thinking?

Canned food is best. If you take the water out of canned food, it will have only 2 to 8 percent carbohydrates, instead of 25 to 50 percent as in dry food. But canned food will have 40 to 55 percent protein, and 20 to 30 percent fat—a good amount of each for a cat. **Canned cat food is the only way to go.**

To add insult to injury, since cats aren't good water drinkers, that dry food has to find water somewhere to re-moisturize itself while it's sitting in the cat's stomach (like gravel), so it sucks fluid from other systems in the body, throwing everything out of whack. For instance, the urine will concentrate even further than normal to conserve water, leading to bladder problems—like stones and sludge, etc.

(By the way, we have found that forcing a pill down a cat often results in the pill remaining lodged in the esophagus for significant amounts of time, until the cat eats something to push it down.

After pilling a cat force a little water, or broth, down him, or her, to help them swallow the pill.)

Bottom line to all this: **Feed canned food to cats. Or feed fresh homemade food.**

I know, canned food stinks, they waste half of it, or one cat will eat it—the other won't, one gets fat—the other gets skinny. Or, they just lick the juice off.

But if you can change your cat from a high-carb dry, to low-carb canned (or raw, or fresh), you will see an unbelievable change—a rejuvenation. It happens without fail. They become more interactive with family, get more exercise, and even act like kittens again. The need for medications for diabetes, arthritis, vomiting or constipation, chronic diarrhea, urinary problems, coat problems, etc., disappear.

· ·

More cat stuff:

Cats don't have well-developed taste buds and rely heavily on sight and smell for their appetite. (This is why a cat with a cold often quits eating.) So, the smellier the food the better. (Sorry.)

Fish sauces such as clam juice, Vietnamese fish sauce, or other fishy odoriferous spreads, or sauces, sometimes attract cats.

Cats generally don't eat fish in the wild, as they are not good at fishing, and generally have an aversion to water. Fish never has been a natural diet for cats. But some cats really love fish. Mercury and selenium can be elevated in a cat's body from too much fish in the diet, causing a vitamin K deficiency, and blood-clotting problems.

The pet industry came up with the idea that cats naturally *crave* fish. They don't. The industry made it up because fish is cheap and easy to process. Additionally, after filleting a fish, there is still lots of the meat left on the bones. Then there are the heads and guts, so, they grind it up for cat food, resulting in too much ash (bone). Additionally, there are species of fish that are incredibly abundant, but that humans don't like to eat. So… "let's feed it to cats."

Fresh or canned fish once or twice a week won't hurt. Some cats relish it. It can be a way to get them to try different foods.

In general cats end up choosing one or two diets and ignore other offerings. This would be fine if those two were mice and birds. So, you will have to experiment for a while until you get them started. (Note: Start them as a kitten.)

Some cats seem to be on a 28-hour feeding schedule instead of 24, so the occasional declining of food is normal. (Sounds typical cat, doesn't it?)

You might be surprised at the interest your cat may show to organ (as opposed muscle) meat. I have seen cats who love (and do well on) raw kidney and liver from cows, pigs, and poultry. Cut the organs into bite-sized pieces raw, and stand back. Also, cold cuts such as sliced chicken, turkey, and beef are often relished. Raw chicken thighs and wings are fine too. It may be disgusting to see your registered pure white longhaired Persian (Fabio) blissed out, smacking down some raw kidney. But hey, that's their inner cat.

Cooking for some cats works best with blenders or food processors. Already puréed meat **baby foods** make a great starting point for switching your cat to wet food, whether canned or homemade. (There is nothing wrong with feeding meat baby food all the time.) Pick the smelliest. Occasionally use the meat ones with veggies.

Worst case: At least supplement dry food with canned or fresh food. There are some decent commercial cat foods on the market. You have to hunt for them in specialty stores. You won't find them in most grocery stores. The basic thing to look for is low, low carbs and high protein and fat. (*Fancy Feast,* canned, is not bad.)

Cats are finicky and creatures of habit. So, start them young, or you'll have to start them old anyway (diabetes). Right now, today, start them on a fresh, grain-free, high-protein-and-fat diet. If they won't eat anything but their grain-based dry food…you are in trouble. You are headed to the vet with a fat cat with medical problems. (See next chapter.) The vet is not going to be able to fix it until you do something about the diet. So why not do something about the diet now?

Cats are supposed to have a discernible waist. Not big fat pads swinging between their back legs as they trot. Get them off carbs. Get them on animal protein and fat.

Experiment with eggs. They are a complete, balanced little bundle of nutrition. Cats are so-so about them when domesticated. You may be able to sneak an egg into the meat as it cooks. You may be able to grate some into the veggie medley described below. Some cats will eat them cooked in butter, or lard (pig fat). Or duck fat. (Use duck fat for cooking yourself—unbelievable!)

I would recommend offering your cat anything and everything. You might be surprised. I am, every day, by what people tell me their cats eat. They have been reported to consume blueberries, tomato juice, clam broth, spaghetti, avocado, cottage cheese, yogurt, milk, cream, bacon, peas, sprouts….

As mentioned before, fish is not a natural diet for cats (but neither is ricotta ravioli), but hey, once or twice a week—go for it.

Try a chicken pot pie. I know cats that live on them too.

What the cat doesn't eat, the dog will.

Let's cook for cats: This is even simpler than making dog food. Basically, you are giving them **meat**, **fat**, and maybe finely grated or minced **vegetables**.

The key is to make a fairly tasteless grated or finely minced vegetable medley, which you add to any meat and fat combination. That's it.

Vegetable Medley: grate or finely mince, then steam, or simmer, in chicken or beef broth, any combination of the following: carrots, sweet potatoes, squash, cauliflower, asparagus, parsley, bamboo shoots, beansprouts, wheat germ, oatmeal, mushrooms, cabbage, kelp, beans, pumpkin, chickpea, spinach, watercress, eggplant, mushrooms, kale, peas, etc. Some cats find the taste of butter, lard (pig fat), or duck fat wonderful and will eat anything cooked in it.

Making them eat vegetables is not mandatory, so don't get hung up on this. It's good but sometimes hard to get them to eat.

Recipe ONE

Ground, or finely chopped, beef, chicken, pork, or turkey, and cook it by any method you want, like a medium-rare steak—lightly cooked, not dry and tough. You can also use rabbit, deer, squirrel, pheasant, quail, animal organ meats, etc. Leave the fat in, or drain part, if there is really too much. Sprinkle a tablespoon or two of your vegetable medley on the meat. That's it.

(By the way, a pressure cooker is a wonderful way to cook pet food. It is incredibly fast and locks in everything from the food while combining the flavors wonderfully. For yourself, try cooking some cheap porkchops—need the fat and bones for flavor—and a can of sauerkraut in the pressure cooker, then serve with mashed potatoes. You're talking maybe ten minutes.)

Recipe TWO

Cook, or open a can (in oil), of anything from the sea. Mackerel, tuna, white fish/cod, salmon, crab, lobster, shrimp, oysters, clams; it doesn't matter, then dust in your veggie medley, stand back. Maybe. Some eat it/some don't. That's it—again, simple. Totally unpredictable as to whether they will eat it or not.

Canned fish cat food is often made from fish parts humans won't eat like bone, scales, eyeballs, heads, fins, etc. So, it is not good. Canned fish cat food costs about the same as our canned tuna. Hmm? So, why not just buy the human tuna.

Recipe THREE

Eggs, cheese, butter, cottage cheese or plain yogurt, milk/cream, catnip (for fun/optional), and your vegetable medley—in any combination your cat will eat, scrambled and cooked lightly. Serve warm or at room temperature. You can add any meat source to this, either to entice the cat, or broaden their diet.

Recipe FOUR
Boil or bake whole chicken in chicken broth. Add minced carrots, yellow squash, zucchini, broccoli, green beans, peas, parsley— in any combination. Add a tablespoon of olive oil, tablespoon of butter, and several tablespoons of cream.

Recipe FIVE
Cut up raw liver or kidney and put it on a plate.

Recipe SIX
Open a can of salmon and put it on a plate.

Recipe SEVEN
Open a can of chicken and put it on a plate.

Recipe EIGHT
Simmer chicken livers, necks, hearts, and gizzards, in chicken broth. Add some of your vegetable medley. Dice or blend. Put it on a plate.

Recipe NINE
Make a meatloaf. Ground meat of any kind or combination, with eggs, cottage cheese, mixed minced vegetables. If lean meats are used add butter, cream, a can of mushroom soup, fish oil, duck fat—anything to make it tastier and more attractive. You getting this? Meat, fat, a little vegetable material. Simple. Did I ever mention corn? No. (Although a little corn and butter and cream... why not?)

And finally, cats like grass. Why? Some theorize it is for the folic acid. Others say it is a natural laxative. Others say, since they can't digest it, it is often thrown back up, which helps cleanse the stomach of other non-digestible stuff they have eaten, like hairballs. Others say cats eat grass to help dislodge post-nasal drainage in the back of their throat. Some will eat beansprouts. Others like it if you grow wheat or oats for them. Even grass seed sprouts grown in a little dirt. Why not? In the wild they would eat the vegetable material in their prey's stomach and intestine. I think they just like the taste.

CHAPTER 8

OBESITY

This may be the most important chapter in the book!

We all know what a lean human looks like. We know what an overweight human looks like. But most of us don't know what a lean canine or feline looks like because it seems they all are fat. A cat or a dog without a waist is considered normal these days. If a puppy isn't roly-poly, you may be reproached of not feeding him or her enough. Very few pets exercise at all. If they do, they are such good athletic specimens, even if overweight, they don't burn off fat. They rarely get cardiac disease, even if twice their ideal weight. But they break down in many other ways.

Cats are not supposed to have fat hanging down between their back legs swinging like a dairy cow headed to the milking parlor.

Dogs are not supposed to have big gobs of fat on their chest, shoulders, and rump.

Our pets are supposed to look like a coyote, or a mountain lion (in the wild—not at a zoo).

There are some breeds that come out of the womb programmed to get fat. They literally have a genetic predisposition to obesity, or overeating. (Dachshunds have been known to still be eating three days after pronounced dead!)

But mostly it is their diet to blame for them being obese. Both the diet itself and the diet's lack of ability to satisfy. With high-carb diets pets don't get satiated. Normal canines and felines eat until satisfied, then fast until hungry again. Not our pets. We just plain feed the wrong diet, and we feed too much of it. They act addicted to it. And we encourage their overeating by showing our "love" using food. Our bond to our pets uses food as currency to pay for their love and show our love. But we are killing our pets in the name of love. In a bazaar twist of irony, we are actually guilty of loving our pets to death.

The biggest single medical problem we see in veterinary medicine in the U.S. today is obesity. In humans, obesity is the second-highest risk factor for cancer, behind tobacco. Since pets don't use tobacco, that probably makes obesity the number-one highest risk factor for cancer for them.

Different studies estimate that from between 30 to 70 percent of family pets in the United States are overweight. Obesity almost always leads to organ failure, as well as musculoskeletal failure. Also, obesity begets obesity; they just get fatter and fatter. It's way better to never get fat in the first place.

Countless disease processes reverse with the shedding of weight. Those pet owners who follow our recommendations for nutrition changes and weight loss always see a betterment of condition and vitality...and the decreased need for medicine. An overabundance of body fat causes a cascade of events that results in diseased organs and systems.

In cats, obesity has been linked with cancer, dental disease, dermatologic diseases, diabetes, liver failure, and lower urinary tract problems.

In dogs, obesity has been linked with diabetes, pancreatitis, cruciate ligament failure, hypothyroidism, hyperadrenocorticism (Cushing's Disease), lower urinary tract disease, oral disease, neoplasia, osteoarthritis, hypertension, altered kidney function, musculoskeletal problems, respiratory distress from obstruction, pregnancy complications, delayed wound healing, increased anesthetic risk, and reduced life expectancy.

Being fat causes a **continuous inflammatory state.** Inflammation is characterized by pain, swelling, heat, adhesions, necrosis, changes in cell walls of various vessels, and an accumulation of fluids. The inflammation from obesity is a response by the body to the lack of blood and oxygen supply to the muscles and organs and, ironically, to the fat tissue itself. It causes a higher level of cortisol than normal in the bloodstream, simulating a daily intake of cortisone (just as if they were taking prednisone every day).

Neutering and spaying maybe reduces energy requirements by 15%. About the time we neuter or spay a pet, their nutritional need for growth is waning, yet we pour on the feed bag, causing obesity, but blaming the surgical procedure.

Additionally, most food labels recommend too much quantity. A good rule of thumb is feed two-thirds of what is recommended on the bag. (And supplement with fresh whole foods.)

Fat isn't stored just under the skin. It coats and surrounds the in- testines, liver, heart, kidneys, etc. One pound of fat may literally have miles of capillaries in it, causing an extra load on the heart especially in times of injury (shock), stress, and disease.

Fat in the chest limits lung expansion and compresses the windpipe. Fat compresses the kidneys. Fat is found packed into almost every nook and cranny in the mammalian body, even in the joints and behind the eyeballs. It completely encases the heart and intestines. It is between muscle layers. It is in the joints. When opening an obese cadaver, you can't even see the heart, kidneys, or intestines for the fat!

In one study, overfed dogs averaged an unbelievable weight gain of 43% in only eight months. (If you weigh 120 pounds, this would be the same as you gaining 53 pounds in eight months.)

So, it is sometimes just a matter of months for a pet to become seriously overweight. I see it every day. "Well, we just didn't get much exercise this winter." "Wow, I don't believe he weighs that much!" "We haven't changed the diet." "We'll start walking again." Hey, pet owners—it's about overeating, not exercise. It's about carbs, not exercise. It's about treats, not exercise. (Four large Milk Bones for a 50-60-pound dog is plenty for a whole day's caloric needs.)

The function of fat traditionally is to be energy storage, thermal insulation, and structural support for some organs. We now know fat tissue is metabolically active and constitutes the largest endocrine[25] organ in the body, and it has unlimited growth potential at any stage of life. It is not inert. It is doing things. Bad things.

Fat begets fat. Fat makes you fatter. No other organ in the body has the potential to grow in mass as fast as fat tissue. No other organ in the body can double the body's weight and still keep growing indefinitely. No other organ in the body can grow indefinitely.

What is actually happening during the "cascade of events" in the body caused by obesity? The following is a step-by-step explanation:

1. The inflammatory state caused by fat excess reduces insulin action in the muscles so the muscle cells don't get the glucose they need to run their metabolic processes.

2. That leads to increased liver production of glucose because the cells are screaming for glucose, but that glucose doesn't get where it is needed, so instead accumulates in the bloodstream.

---

25 The endocrine system is the system of glands that secretes different types of hormones into the bloodstream. These hormones influence almost every cell, organ, and function of our bodies. Some of the hormones secreted by fat cells called adipocytes are a group of proteins called adipokines. These exert their effect in the central nervous system and in tissue such as skeletal muscle and the liver. Additionally, many pro-cytokines and acute-phase proteins originate in adipocytes. Leptin, adiponectin, resistin, visfatin, retinol-binding protein, and tumor necrosis factor-alpha are some of the main adipokines. Leptin concentrations increase with increased body fat in all species, including dogs and cats. Leptin functions to reduce appetite. But leptin resistance develops with increasing obesity.

3. This increase of glucose in the bloodstream leads to the pancreas making more insulin because the body is yelling, "Get this glucose out of my bloodstream," and that leads to too much insulin in the bloodstream.

4. But the insulin isn't getting to the cells, where it is needed, because of the inflammatory state. This limits the ability of the cells to burn stored fat (lipolysis).

5. So, less fat is being burned, so it's getting harder and harder to lose weight. Also, the fat actually starts getting hard and dense (and different colors—like brown and yellow—yuck).

6. Hard fat begins to accumulate inside the arteries and joints (causing arthritis and atherosclerosis). It accumulates hidden between belly muscle layers.

7. The partially fat-clogged arteries include the coronary arteries (they provide the blood supply to the heart), so this causes damage to the heart—even heart cell death.

8. The damaged/diseased/unhappy heart reduces output, so everybody suffers on down the line with a further lack of oxygen and nutrients. Everything downstream feels inflamed and quits doing their job due to lack of nutrients for energy and oxygen.

9. Finally, the pancreas may just give up, exhausted from the increased insulin production, and diabetes ensues. There is still plenty of glucose—the liver soldiers on making it—but the glucose can't get to the cells to be converted into the most important chemical in the body made by the mitochondria powerhouses that are in the nucleus of each cell. That important chemical is called adenosinetryphosphate, or ATP. ATP drives every metabolic process in the body. It's

been called the "molecular unit of currency" of intercellular transfer of energy. Without insulin no ATP gets made.

10. By this time there may be irreversible damage all over the body. The liver is opting out of the game. The kidneys are getting squashed in the dark, wondering what is happening— some of their cells start to die—urea begins to back up instead of being converted to ammonia and excreted out the urinary tract. The bladder can't hold much anyway—no room because of accumulated fat—so urine leaks out during sleep, resulting in chronic bladder infections. The heart is sick (literally) of working so hard trying to keep things together. The lungs are literally collapsing (atelectasis). **Even the fat tissue itself isn't all that happy**.

11. The cycle keeps repeating itself, and the disease state intensifies.

12. Eventually the kidneys quit making a hormone called angiotensin that is required to make red blood cells. Now red blood cell production is reduced adding insult to injury, and results in anemia.

13. So, even less oxygen is getting where it needs to go due to lack of red blood cells.

14. As if this wasn't enough damage, many aspects of tumor promotion arise from the persistent and unresolved inflammation due to obesity. This includes cancers of the breast, ovarian, colon, rectum, lungs, liver, prostate, bladder, pancreas, and of course (ironically) cancer of the fat.

15. Finally, multiple complications ensue—take your pick: chronic obstructive disease of the intestine, asthma, obstructive sleep apnea, obesity-hypoventilation syndrome, stroke, benign

and malignant gastrointestinal diseases, gallbladder disease, thyroid disease, polycystic ovary disease, hyperuricemia (gout), urinary stone disease, joint degradation from excess weight bearing and inflammation, immunity failure so viruses and other microbes, as well as aberrant cancer cells may be uncontrolled resulting in pop-up tumors or infections anywhere, heat stroke, gangrene, and on and on.

There is very little of the body that is left unaffected by obesity. Obesity, this excess of fat, causes the whole organism to react in a pathological way, just as an injury or infection would—but pathology you can't get rid of. A disease you can't cure. It keeps on destroying. It keeps on growing. It is a monster.

Obesity makes the doctor's job complicated since nothing really can be done to reverse the damage being caused…except get rid of the fat. Surgery is incredibly difficult in the obese patient. The fat cells literally burst, releasing slippery oil that slimes instruments and gloves during surgery, not to mention the general weakness in the tissues all over the body caused by that tissue being infused with fat. Suture material won't hold in fat. Obesity profoundly interferes with wound healing as well.

In summary, obesity causes biochemical changes that result in an increased susceptibility to other diseases. Weight loss reverses many of the changes that occur with obesity. If it is not too late.

Managing weight loss in pets:
In humans there is a 95% failure rate in weight loss attempts. In one dog study, in a controlled university setting, there was only a 50% success rate. (Did you get that? Even at the university level, diets fail!) Better to not store the fat in the first place.

Dogs don't lose weight by exercising. They only lose weight by reducing caloric intake. No matter what you do, you still have to reduce calories to lose weight in a dog. Maintaining the ideal weight after dieting is helped by continuing exercise. Exercise can make more muscle to replace fat.

All overweight dogs have to undergo behavior modification. Everyone in the family has to be on board with the program or it will fail. That is, begging, and equating food with love has to stop. Exercise will help maintain and even increase muscle mass while burning fat. The goal is to lose fat, not muscle. I've had dogs not lose weight—just rearrange their weight by adding muscle. They are born athletes and will bulk up muscle if they exercise. Exercise gives them something to do, and makes them feel better, and is good for the owner as well.

As with people, losing weight is all about counting calories. It always involves a lifestyle change to lose weight. And it takes time. Crash diets don't work in the long run. Sometimes we lose a little weight, and then plateau at that new weight, making the whole process discouraging. Then we give up (again). Dogs sometimes will plateau for months, then start losing weight again as the body's metabolism changes permanently. Fortunately for the dog, since he doesn't have the key to the refrigerator, his weight loss diet doesn't take any willpower on his part.

Weight-loss diets often just contain added indigestible fiber (cellulose as in paper), hoping that the feeling of a full stomach will aid in the dog losing weight. It can work sometimes, but there are better ways than feeding paper. Besides, all you get is a voluminous stool. Or worse—gas-forming bacteria eat on the fiber, resulting in your dog peeling paint with flatulence. I know they'll eat anything, but paper? Come on.

If you're cooking for your dog, reducing calories is easy. Just be careful with the fat and carbohydrates, feed plenty of lean protein, and increase the amount of vegetables. Rice helps because it requires fat to be digestible.

It's okay to feed treats. In fact, give them all they want. But only what I call "conscious-free" treats. These are treats with a near-zero-calorie content. Use vegetables soaked in beef or chicken broth—carrots, green beans, lima beans, cabbage, zucchini, squash, or any other kind of vegetable you want. Keep the jar of broth and veggies soaking in the refrigerator. Sometimes it helps acceptability if you parboil the vegetables first. (Parboiling is just barely cooking the vegetable so the outside is soft and full of flavor, but the inside still stays crunchy.) The salt in the broth won't hurt them; it may increase their water consumption, which is necessary for burning fat.

Another treat: rice cakes (they look like a hockey puck) dipped in beef or chicken broth. Rice actually requires fat to metabolize so "sucks" fat out of the body. Tasty but low cal.

Toast with a thin coating of peanut butter is satisfying. The peanut butter gets stuck on the roof of their mouth and they are "satisfied" because they have to smack their lips for a while.

Dry crackers dipped in a little fat-free unsweetened yogurt works. Or dry crackers by themselves.

You get the picture. Reduce the calories, increase exercise, eat lots of veggies, and drink lots of water. Feed a diet with little fat, low carbs, and high protein. This is nothing new. An overweight human has to do exactly the same thing.

There is a "magic pill" now for dogs. It is called **Slentrol** (dirlotapide). It causes an increased accumulation of triglycerides in the cells lining the intestine (enterocytes). This results in a secretion of satiety hormones, leading to a voluntary decrease in caloric intake. It also reduces fat absorption. Sorry, it doesn't work on humans (or cats). Check with your vet. Tests will have to be run and the drug is a pricy. Slentrol just makes it a little easier on the dog.

Dogs have varied responses to Slentrol. Some lose weight quickly because of a greatly reduced appetite. Others maintain their appetite right through the treatment. Occasionally some will actually gain weight.

Slentrol can be useful if the dog is unable to move about much, such as post-knee-repair surgery, or being too heavy to exercise comfortably. During a weight-loss program using Slentrol, do not feed a low-calorie food, as the drug works best with a higher fat intake.

As the ideal weight is approached and Slentrol is stopped, the dog's appetite will increase and weight may rebound. It is important to transition the dog to a lower total calorie intake when the course of treatment is finished. Again, keeping weight off requires a lifestyle change with everyone in the family being on board with the program.

Feline Obesity and treatment for:
The normal cat should be well-proportioned, have an observable waist behind the ribs, ribs palatable with slight fat covering, and a minimal abdominal fat pad between the back legs.

Over one-third (some studies say over one-half) of cats are overweight. I think its 90%—unless they are kittens. In fact, most cat-owning clients I see believe that a cat whose ribs are not palatable, whose waist is poorly discernible and with an obvious rounding of the abdomen, and that have a hanging fat pad between the back legs is normal. Sorry, it's not. When we X-ray these cats, we see an eight-pound cat in a twelve-pound body. The skeleton is dwarfed by fat tissue. And yet they are still very athletic. Imagine you carrying around a cinder block or two, everywhere you go— see how climbing stairs would go. They can still jump on the counter even with the "cinder blocks."

Because of the metabolic requirement for cats to use protein exclusively as an energy source, carbohydrates go directly to obesity jail, confined for life to a fat "cell" in "Adipose Prison."

Interestingly real weight loss is not accomplished in cats using the traditional energy restriction (decreased calories) diet. This does lead to weight loss, but to the detriment of lean body mass (muscle). They lose muscle too. A successful weight-loss program leads to fat loss, while keeping muscle mass. The lack of lean body mass (muscle) assures a rapid regain of weight, only it will be fat again if they go back to the high-carb diet. *Unless you feed high protein and low carbs*, the lean body mass will still be absent and fat will again accumulate. Satiation will not be satisfied and appetite not reduced. They will eat compulsively.

By the way, never impose a "crash diet" on a cat (total fasting/ star-vation). This causes some of the fat not to be burned but instead be transferred and stored in the liver, resulting in a condition called feline hepatic lipidosis, or "fatty-liver syndrome." It is usually fatal. It does lead to a rapid weight loss because they just quit eating entirely and have to be force fed, usually by stomach tube.

So, in any weight-loss program for fat cats, it is essential that they be fed a diet high in protein. Canned food is the best because of the high meat protein, low carbohydrate content, and high-water content. Home cooking is ideal.

By the way, it is interesting to note that around 50 percent of diabetic cats recover from diabetes when put on a proper diet of high protein and low carbohydrates, and if they lose weight. It can take a year. Often it is not too late to have the pancreas start making insulin again after the disease process of obesity is halted and reversed.

There are weight loss diets for cats. They work if you totally make the switch and feed nothing else. Feeding Hill's Prescription Diet® feline r/d® has been shown to reduce cats' body fat by 30 percent in 4 months. It does work if the owner is totally committed and the fat cat can be kept away from the skinny cat's food.

Cats won't eat vegetable treats usually. Many will eat sliced beef, chicken, or turkey cold-cuts. This is a perfect treat for a cat. It can be hard to live with a cat on a diet.

It's practically impossible to put one cat on a diet in a multiple-cat household. In these circumstances just switch to a high-protein, low-carb diet. Cats become satiated quickly on those diets and actually start losing weight without a weight-loss program.

ALWAYS take away the bowl of dry kibble. Feed only canned

food and small amounts of cold-cuts. They will cry and moan but you have to do it.

It's better to never let them gain the weight in the first place. From day one NO DRY FOOD AT ALL. It can be like poison.

I know cats are very popular pets largely because they are easy to keep; leave a bowl of dry kibble out, and change the litter box occasionally. But we have been paying for convenience with obesity, and all the health issues associated with it. They are obligatory carnivores. They simply cannot be healthy on high-carbohydrate diets. Try going canned, formulating your own food, or at least supplementing as much as possible with baby food, cold-cuts, canned meats, and all the cat-feeding suggestions in this book.

Or…raise parakeets.

CHAPTER 9

MYTHS ABOUT FEEDING PETS

Dogs should not be fed table scraps:
I think we have already dispelled that myth. Pet food manufacturers perpetuate this notion, explaining scraps will upset the balance of the commercial dog food. Pets do not require a diet that provides uniform meals every day any more than people do.

Begging, getting fat, and not eating their food, is not due to feeding table scraps. It is a lifestyle problem. Our pets can be manipulative creatures. They train us to respond to begging. Besides, who wants to eat kibble when you can have steak? If you give table foods as a treat, at least use them as training tool. Make them do something to get the treats. And don't feed them when you eat if you don't want them begging constantly and shamelessly. On the other hand, if that is your style...share your food. Make extra. Go for it.

Testimonials:
A lot of so-called experts don't know what they are talking about.

Pet food authors and reviewers (into "raw," or "keto," or any other type of faddish diet) are often just selling books, actually working for specific manufactures, or selling advertising on their website. Or they may just be nut-cases.

Some so-called "experts" have been known to rank new pet-food companies high that don't disclose their ingredient sources and use generic co-packers, but rank low those with decades of experience, excellent records of ingredient high quality, and that run their own facilities. They are often biased simply because they are working for a pet food marketing department in some way. They may be completely phony like an actor on TV dressed up as a doctor selling a weight-loss product. Whatever…you can say anything you want in the pet food industry. (See Chapter 3.)

"The addition of glucosamine and chondroitin in dog food is proven." The truth is you can't put enough of those in pet food to make any difference.

Often a certain ingredient is touted as being superior to the type used by other manufacturers. For instance, the claim *"Brown rice is better and more natural than white rice."* Actually, brown rice is higher in fiber and ash than white rice, which has had the bran layer removed, making the white rice easier to digest and less irritating to the stomach. Really, it doesn't matter. Just cook it well. (There are hundreds of types of rice in the world. A better solution is to feed a diverse variety of rice.)

Ignore testimonials in general. Remember, no one has to actually provide proof for any statement about anything in the pet food industry. (See Chapter 3.) A zealot breeder can be the worst so-called expert—many make up for ignorance with punctuating their nutty notions with vehement certainty.

Raw food is what animals eat in the wild:
Raw food advocates preach this as near Biblical doctrine. However, wild animals don't live as long, have almost constant diarrhea, eat poisonous and rancid stuff and die, and their choices of foodstuffs are poor. Worms and grubs may be the blue-plate special today. Tomorrow may be bark. The next day acorns, followed by a

dessert of assorted scat.[26]

Evolution is sometimes underrated by those raw-food-only believers. Archeological evidence of fire and cooking date back at least 800,000 years and some argue 1.8 million years. As the companion canine evolved, it ate what we ate, and lived longer and healthier than their wild cousins.

Raw is okay, just very hard to pull off. Do your homework.

Cooking destroys the nutritional value of food:
Very high temperatures overheating protein can lead to reduced protein digestibility, as well as amino acid destruction. Normal cooking causes only decreases the digestibility of protein by 5-7%. Carbohydrate and fat digestibility are improved by cooking. You cannot digest uncooked rice; it has to be cooked. It is well known that antioxidants are more available in cooked foods. Also, moderate heating destroys anti-nutritive enzymes such as trypsin inhibitors present in some protein sources. In uncooked food there may be E. coli, salmonella, listeria, Guardia, staph, etc., which can actually kill you, or make you wish you would die.

Corn and wheat are bad ingredients, they are hard to digest, and are common causes for allergies:
Some individual pets are allergic to corn or wheat. They should not be the main source of protein in dog and cat diets anyway. Whole corn (kernels or ground) is the way to go, not fractions or byproducts of corn processing. Popcorn won't hurt them at all. Canned corn, frozen corn, grits, stuffing…all can be used as a source.

Freezing raw diets kills bacteria:
Most of the bacteria found in raw meat can survive freezing. Additionally, bacteria quickly colonize as the meat thaws. Only cooking can kill bacteria.

---

26 Wild animal poop.

Cooking destroys enzymes needed for digestion:
All the enzymes that dogs and cats need for digestion are already in their gastrointestinal tract. Additional enzymes from food are not required for digestion. In fact, added enzymes are treated by the intestine as just another form of protein and are broken down by the gastrointestinal tract and treated as food. (There is a rare condition where the pancreas quits making digestive enzymes and they have to be taken with food.)

Grains are added to pet foods as fillers:
Whole corn, oats, rice, barley, and other grains are healthy ingredients that contain protein, carbohydrates, fats, vitamins, and minerals. There is nothing wrong with them when used in dog food. It's the lack of animal protein in those foods that is the problem. Also, they have to be cooked. Pulverizing them into a powder first, then cooking them, can rob them of nutritional value. For instance, soybeans should be soaked in its whole configuration, and then cooked. Industrial preparation usually powders it first, and then cooks it.

Beet pulp is a poor-quality filler:
It actually is a good source for the beneficial bacteria in the intestine. It is a "probiotic." It is a gentle source of fiber that (friendly) gut bacteria can use. Almost all the sugar in beet pulp is gone by extraction. In fact, there is more sugar in a carrot than in sugar beet pulp.

Fresh vegetables and fruit are better than frozen or canned:
Kansas State University School of Agriculture found that the nutritional value between fresh, frozen, and canned was identical. In fact, many frozen and canned foods actually outperformed the fresh because they were picked at peak ripeness, and had not deteriorated during shipping and storage, or while on the shelf.[27]

---

27 Karen Blakeslee, www.ksre.ksu.edu/sty/2007/cannedorfrozen020607.htm.

Texture may change from freezing and thawing. Salt and sugar may be added in excess in canned foods. Freezing does not preserve food as long as canning. But all in all, for you and your pets, canned and frozen fruits and vegetables are just as good as fresh.

Canned and frozen may not be as good tasting as real organic or fresh. Buy veggies and fruit in the summer at their peak, locally grown by known organic farmers (Amish, for instance) and freeze, and can them yourselves.

Dogs should not be fed raw eggs:
There is an enzyme called avidin in the egg white that destroys biotin. Biotin is known as vitamin H, or co-enzyme R. A deficiency in biotin can lead to hair loss, conjunctivitis, and dermatitis. Eating only egg whites can cause the deficiency too. Cooking denatures avidin so it can't destroy biotin. But it doesn't matter because if you eat the *whole* raw egg, yolk included, the problem is eliminated because the yoke supplies more than enough biotin, thereby offsetting the biotin destroying avidin in the white. (This is a perfect example of why we should eat whole foods, not parts of foods. The contents in whole foods are meant to work together.)

Cooking eggs to prevent the chance of a salmonella intestinal infection is the best reason not to feed raw eggs. Chickens can pass salmonella from their vent[28] onto their eggs.

Dogs and cats have short gastrointestinal tracts so they won't get infections from salmonella:
The gastrointestinal tract of dogs is not shorter compared to people's G.I. tract when viewed in proportion to their smaller body size. Cats, however, do have a shorter intestinal tract so they need high-density proteins and fats. Dogs and cats can become infected with salmonella and other bacteria found in raw foods, just as people

---

28 Birds have a "vent," which allows for the passage of eggs, and kidney and intestinal waste, through the same port as opposed to having a separate vagina, penis, and rectum. Therefore, contamination of the egg with feces from the hen is common.

can, especially the young, old, and immunosuppressed. Dogs do have a very acidic stomach, and food stays in their stomachs longer than in human stomachs, thereby destroying harmful microbes. But, it's still better not to take them in anyway. Cook the food.

Dogs need a food appropriate for their life stage:
Pet food manufacturers made this up. Thanks, marketing. The more items of one brand on the shelf, the higher the visibility, the higher the sales. Regular dog food is fine for puppies and seniors. Puppies eat more. Seniors eat less. Senior specific diets often have more filler fiber in them, assuming the senior is prone to obesity, or constipation. In fact, the senior dog and cat may need less fiber and a better protein. I have suggested using puppy food for older dogs having trouble with not getting enough to eat. (Think *Ensure.*) Also—humans may need fiber. Dogs and cats don't.

A dog's digestive tract is not able to digest grains.
They can't digest the starch in raw grains. But they can digest cooked grains. Cooked rice is almost all digested whereas wheat and corn end up with about 20% not absorbed. (That contributes to flatulence because gas producing bacteria feed on the undigested grain.)

I've always fed my dogs this and they did fine:
The dog food companies change their formulas and ingredients often, usually not improving it at all—just making it more economically advantageous for them. Besides, as a vet, seeing thousands of dogs, your dogs are actually not "fine." Feed a high-quality diet and watch them get a spring back in their step, and increase their activity and playfulness. Skin allergy symptoms may disappear, muscle tone improves, their coat gets glossier and denser, skin odor and flatulence disappear, and they will have better breath.

You should never give chicken bones to dogs:
Raw chicken bones are well tolerated by dogs. Cooked chicken

bones are more brittle and when they break, they have sharp ends so are not recommended. Also, chicken bones baked at low temperatures overnight, as explained in the dog food chapter, are fairly digestible, and don't splinter. When in doubt, don't feed chicken bones. (Or rib bones from pigs and cows.)

Fat is bad for dogs:
Fats are highly digestible, tasty, and are more energy dense than protein or carbohydrates. (One gram of fat supplies 2.4 times the energy from one gram of protein or carbohydrates.) Fat is a source for vitamins A, D, E, and K, and what are called the essential fatty acids (essential, means the body is not able to manufacture them itself). Fat is also a metabolic source of water; hardworking dogs won't dehydrate as fast when fed a diet high in fat.

Pork is bad for dogs:
It is the fat. Pork can be fatty. Trim off the fat and dogs and cats do fine on it. Also, they have trouble with chemicals used in curing— the smoke flavor and nitrites. Go easy on the ham and bacon.

CHAPTER 10

SUPPLEMENTS AND NUTRACEUTICALS

A huge industry has been built around the notion that "micronutrients" are either missing (deficiency) in our diets, or if added (supplement), will improve overall health.

It started with salt. Iodine was added to salt to prevent thyroid goiter.

In this day and age, every major nutritional deficiency has been addressed, and is nonexistent in our modern well-fed society. **ALL** we need is found in a **balanced** diet:

- Osteoporosis, rickets, tetany—calcium
- Keshan disease—selenium
- Iron-deficiency anemia
- Growth retardation—zinc
- Beriberi—Thiamine (vitamin B1)
- Pellagra—niacin (vitamin B3)
- Scurvy—vitamin C
- Osteoporosis, rickets—vitamin D
- Night blindness—vitamin A

- Hemophilia—vitamin K
- Folate deficiency—vitamin B9
- Riboflavin deficiency—vitamin B2

Yet over 50,000 supplement products are on the market. They make all kinds of claims: boosts the immune system, retards aging, prevents cancer…and arthritis…and colds, detoxifies the liver…and on and on. You can basically claim anything you want in this industry with impunity.

I am not talking about **functional foods.** These are fortified or enriched during processing, such as adding vitamin D to milk. (And iodine to salt.)

We all know about **vitamins.** Take a *Flintstones* daily and hedge your bets. Not needed…but why not. Vitamin-mineral supplements are very overrated, although literally everyone thinks they are deficient in something. Unless you have a disease that prevents absorption of these things, you're not.

One vitamin, vitamin B12, or cobalamin, is manufactured by flora in a healthy intestine and absorbed into the bloodstream in the colon. With disease, and even old age, the ability to absorb vit B12 can be compromised and will result in pernicious anemia. Older people and animals may benefit from monthly injections of this vitamin. Giving it orally generally is useless, as it is not absorbed.

Any disease condition in dogs and cats can result in deficiencies in vitamins. Therefore, veterinarians routinely give liver extract with B vitamins, iron, etc., by injection, as part of a therapeutic regimen.

Nutraceuticals and **bioceuticals** are supplements that are supposed to be pharmaceutical alternatives, which claim physiological benefits, in a so-called "natural" way. (By the way… many drugs literally come from nature, or were synthesized to do the same thing as nature's version without the side-effects, or will last longer, or have an increased potency.)

The terms "nutraceutical" and "bioceutical" are not defined by U.S. law.

There are thousands of "miraculous" cures, "natural" cures, preventions, and health enhancers being touted as beneficial for all kinds of things: green-lipped mussel extract, deer-velvet, colloidal-silver, kava, country-mallow, chia, horny-goat weed, chaparral...on and on. And on.

Their "benefits" are based on personal accounts, rather than facts, or research. The so-called benefits are purely anecdotal. If you're lucky they won't do harm, and are at least a placebo.

These dietary supplements do not have to be approved by the FDA (Federal Drug Administration) before marketing.[29]

It's a multibillion-dollar industry with powerful connections, but with **woefully inadequate regulation.**[30]

To date, the FDA has banned only one nutraceutical ingredient, ephedrine, that was used in some weight-loss products. And that took ten years even though it clearly caused thousands of adverse reactions and even deaths. Instead of attempting more bans, the FDA now issues warnings, detains imported products, and ask companies for voluntary recalls.

The FDA has taken legal action in only 30 cases against supplement marketers that claimed their products were cures of specific diseases. (Out of over 50,000 products out there.)

FDA rules don't apply to manufacturing quality when companies are supplying herbs, vitamins, and most raw ingredients. Yet supplements containing heavy metals, pesticides, and even prescription drugs are readily available to the unwary. The FDA supposedly was granted authority to combat health fraud by the 1994 Dietary Supplement Health and Education Act (DSHEA).

---

29 Companies must register their manufacturing facilities with the FDA and follow current good manufacturing practices. With a few well-defined exceptions, dietary supplements may only be marketed to support the structure of function of the body, and may not claim to treat a disease or condition, and must include a label that says, "These statements have not been evaluated by the Food and Drug Administration. This product is not intended to diagnose, treat, cure, or prevent any disease." The exceptions are when the FDA has reviewed and approved a health claim.

30 Dannon Yogurt was forced to pay millions for falsely claiming its products Actimel and Activia boosted the immune system.

But, **consumer-freedom concerns, and protests,** have hamstrung the FDA. They only get involved if there is a problem, not for prevention of a problem. An individual has the "right to put whatever they want in their own body" is the basis for no government regulation or enforcement.

Safety, efficacy, dosage, quality control—the rock-bottom agenda for the FDA to approve a drug—is completely missing in the massive supplement/nutraceutical industry.

Let's look at them one at a time:

1. Safety

Supplement manufactures don't have to demonstrate that their products are safe. Even though:

- *Colloidal silver* turns skin permanently blue.
- Excess *selenium* causes hair loss, and toenails and fingernails to fall off.
- Body-building supplements with *synthetic steroids* have turned eyes yellow and caused liver failure.
- Aphrodisiac/erectile enhancement formulas containing *yohimbine* have caused heart failure.
- *Germanium* used for glaucoma and HIV treatment has caused kidney failure.
- *Chaparral* used for colds, weight loss, cancer, and detoxification has destroyed kidneys and livers.
- *Comfrey* used for heavy menstrual periods, and nearly everything else, has caused cancer and liver damage.
- *Kava* for anxiety has caused liver damage. (Is banned in Germany, Switzerland, and Canada.)
- *Lobelia* as a stop-smoking aid, and for asthma, has caused cardiac fibrillation, bottoming out blood pressure, comas, and death.
- *Coltsfoot* for cough, sore throat, laryngitis, bronchitis, and asthma has caused liver damage and cancer.

- *Bitter orange* for weight loss, congestion, and allergies has caused heart attack, stroke, and death.
- *Country mallow* for weight loss, allergies, and detoxification has caused heart attacks and strokes.

Adverse effects are estimated by the *Adverse Events Reporting System* to be linked to 12% of supplements.

2. Efficacy

Of the more than 54,000 supplement products in the *Natural Medicines Comprehensive Database* (NMCD), only about one-third have some level of effectiveness supported by scientific evidence. It is impossible to do double-blind studies (placebo verses actual product) on products containing multiple ingredients.

The rest of efficacy claims are purely anecdotal.

Even though it is against the law for companies to claim that any supplement can prevent, treat, or cure any disease other than a nutrient-deficiency condition, the practice is rampant. Once undercover investigators from the *Government Accountability Office*, posing as elderly consumers, caught sales personnel claiming that their garlic supplement could be taken in lieu of high blood pressure medicine.

3. Dosage

I have seen recommended doses of vitamins that vary from 5 to 1600 iu/day. Optimal, or safe, doses of supplements are rarely known for animals. At best they are based on the amount given to humans. Supplementing various pet species is clearly an experiment.

The overdosing of vitamins is worse than underdosing. Overdoses of vitamin A, E, and beta-carotene have been linked to peeling skin, hair loss, stomach upset, diarrhea, nausea, bleeding, blurred vision, and fatigue and weakness.

Giving isolated single ingredients may deplete another substance in the body, causing a new problem.

Then there are adverse drug reactions of supplements interacting with prescription drugs.

4. Quality Control

Tests by *Consumerlab.com* found high rates of problems in 3,000 products it has tested since 1999.[31] **"One out of four either doesn't contain what it claims, or has contamination. Or the pills won't break apart properly,"** said company president Tod Cooperman. One "gummy bear" calcium product had 250% of the vitamin D claimed on the label. Another liquid product made with rose hips had half the amount of vit C it claimed.

Consumer Lab found fourteen brands of *glucosamine* (see below: Do they work?) to have between 59% to 130% of what the label stated.

In another study they found that three *sustained-release* products released 90% in just four hours. Some didn't release any at all in twelve hours. And release times varied from pill to pill *in the same bottle!*

Another study of *probiotics* ("beneficial bacteria") found two of the thirteen products tested contained *no actual bacteria.* Another had 250% of the stated amount. And this next fact would be funny if it wasn't pathetic: 39% of the so-called microorganisms in one probiotic product *didn't exist!* The names were made up!

Supplements: Do they work *in pets*? Some discussed:

1. Glucosamine

On its own or in combination with chondroitin, methylsulfonylmethane (MSM), mussel extract, and hundreds of other ingredients. Decades of clinical trials have failed to find any consistent benefit in humans and there have been only two clinical

---

31 Consumerlab.com tests dietary supplements for purity, potency, bioavailability, etc. It requires a paid subscription to check for reviewed products. Worth considering before taking, or giving your pets, any supplement.

trials done on dogs with no benefit found. The non-steroidal anti-inflammatory (NSAID) therapy usually accompanying the use of chondroitin was a constant feature in the trials—which it is believed was responsible for all the pain relief attained. One study using glucosamine for treatment of cat cystitis found no evidence of benefit either.

(Injectable glucosamine has been effective in horses.)

2. Fish Oil

Cats and dogs don't have problems with cardiovascular disease, a common use of fish oils in humans. There has been some evidence that fish oil supplements improve coat quality in animals, but there is no specific source, dosage, or formulation that is better than others. There have been several studies concerning fish oil benefits for arthritis in dogs but found only some proof of benefit.

Commercial pet diets may have adequate fat-soluble vitamins (A, D, and E) when they leave the factory, but time in storage, and storage conditions, may result in them denaturing before the animal consumes the product. Adding fat-soluble vitamins and essential fatty acids to a dog and cat diet has merit.

3. Probiotics and Prebiotics

The use as therapy for gastrointestinal disease is supported—as in replacing reduced number of gut flora reduced by antibiotics. But many products are marketed with ridiculous and completely unsupported claims. The feeding of unsweetened, non-pasteurized yogurt, for the lactobacillus acidophilus "friendly bacteria," is probably better.

4. Multivitamins

There is no research on dogs and cats supporting the benefit touted by the claims of supplement marketers. Commercial pet foods, and diversified home-cooked diets (with commercial food available) negate any benefit of supplemental multivitamins.

They may, in fact, cause harm. Synthetic vitamin A has been

shown to alter vitamin E levels. Continued taking of synthetic vitamins may actually lead to deficiencies of other essential nutritional factors. A carrot has 500 things in it besides beta-carotene and vitamin A. Why not feed whole cooked carrots? Excess vitamin A can cause vomiting, appetite loss, abdominal pain, dizziness, edema in the brain, rash, peeling skin, hair loss, easy fractures of bones, bulging eyeballs, coma, and death.

Ascorbic acid is commonly thought of as vitamin C, but ascorbic acid is really just a small part of a complex. The other parts of Vitamin-C-Complex include ascorbigen bioflavonoid complexes, tyrosinase, P factors, K factors and J factors, etc. These other "parts" contribute to the integrity of small blood vessels, thyroid and adrenal function, blood clotting, the production of norepinephrine and dopamine, and the oxygen carrying capability of blood cells. Vitamin C complex is found in organ meats, eggs, and dairy products, and carnivorous mammals generally produce their own.

5. Digestive Enzymes:

Healthy humans and pets have all the digestive enzymes they need provided by organs doing what they are supposed to do. Taking enzymes for better digestion, cancer treatment, or anti-inflammatory effects, provide no benefit; they are just digested with the rest of the stuff swallowed. However, pancreatic-insufficiency (diseased, or due to a nonfunctional pancreas) does require three supplemental enzymes: protease, lipase, and amylase to digest protein, carbohydrates, and fat. These are often actually mixed in the food prior to consumption.

The Ratio of Omega-3; Omega-6 Essential Fatty Acids in diet is a REAL problem:

These fatty acids are "essential" because our bodies cannot make them. We have to take them in orally. They should be consumed in a ratio of 1 to 1. But our diets these days are skewed with too much omega-6, and not enough omega-3. Or, in the case of commercial kibble, may have had adequate amounts when it left the factory, but time and conditions during shipping and storage (bag open in your pantry) may have allowed these oils to denature and be no longer efficacious.

Additionally, and **this is important,** if omega-6 is too high, and omega-3 is too low, it results in an "inflammation-precipitator" scenario. High omega-6 causes elevated blood glucose levels, and the creation of inflammatory substances such as prostaglandins, leukotrienes, and free-radicals.

In the last 50 years, the typical Western diet (and commercial pet foods) have 10 to 30 times more omega-6s than omega-3s. This is because of the industrialization of feeding food-producing livestock. When cattle are taken off grass to be "finished" in feedlots on grain, they lose their storage of omega-3s. "Grass-fed" dairy cows' milk and butterfat contain substantially more omega-3s than those in factory farms. Their butter is healthier and softer. The meat from grass-fed cattle, with more omega-3s, tastes better, and is tenderer than that from feedlot cattle.

Eggs from hens that forage on grass and consume insects contain higher omega-3s than those fed corn, milo, and soybeans.

Look at the ratios of omega-3 essential fatty acids to omega-6 essential fatty acids in the oils we commonly consume in our Western diets:

- **Corn oil-** 1 omega-3 to 46 omega-6s
- **Peanut oil-** no omega-3 at all
- **Soybean oil-** 1 omega-3 to 7 omega-6s
- **Canola oil-** 1 omega-3 to 2 omega-6s (not bad)
- **Olive oil-** 1 omega-3 to 13 omega-6s
- **Sunflower oil-** 1 omega-3 to **70** omega-6s
- **Linseed (flaxseed) oil- 3 omega-3s to 1 omega-6.** This is the only one that contains more omega-3 than omega-6! Linseed (flaxseed) cultivated since ancient times was used for bread in Greece and Rome.

When food-producing animals have just a 5% amount of cooked linseed added to their diet, it greatly increases the omega-3s in their meat, dairy products, and eggs.

The Greenland Inuit people consume large amounts of "cold-water" fish (high in omega-3s) and display virtually no cardiovascular disease.

A 2010 study of 3,081 women suffering from breast cancer found that consumption of increased omega-3 fatty acids produced a 25% reduced risk of additional breast cancer events.[32]

Hydrogenated trans-fat made from vegetable oil greatly decreased the incidence of the rancidity of fat and increased shelf life. (*Twinkies* last forever, LOL.) But the industrial and commercial use of the high omega-6 essential fatty acid oils is causing inflammatory diseases and obesity in us and our pets. The consumption of these hydrogenated vegetable oils since World War II has risen 6-fold. (The use of trans-fat has been banned in some places.)

So...cold-water fish oils rich in omega-3 essential fatty acids have been established to provide multiple health benefits both in animals and man.

Bottom line for your pet's nutrition needs:
If you cook for your pet, there is little need to supplement with anything as long as the diet is diverse and whole foods are used. If there is a skin problem, fat-soluble vitamin supplement (A, D, and E) with essential fatty acids may be helpful. (Cold-water fish oils).

If feeding dry kibble only...yes, add fat-soluble vitamins and essential fatty acid supplement. A multivitamin/mineral tablet once a day cannot hurt.

Because there are so many choices out there, I would strongly recommend consulting with your veterinarian for a product recommendation.

---

32 Patterson, R.E et al. (2010). "Marines Fatty Acid Intake is Associated with Breast Cancer Prognosis." *The Journal of Nutrition 141 (2): 201206.*

I would alternate manufacturers as quality can vary even within individual manufacturing facilities.

And if you cannot cook for your pet, at least supplement with fresh animal protein daily. Eggs, cheese, meats, vegetables in some form benefit all pets. Make them an omelet every day. Share your meatloaf. Lasagna. Cottage cheese. Especially a growing animal.

(For a list of vitamins, sources, actions, see Appendix 2.)

CHAPTER 11

FINALLY! THE END

DO NOT BE AFRAID TO GIVE YOUR PET HUMAN FOOD! (See the section of foods you cannot give.)

If you can't cook for your pets, at least give them a variety of whole foods daily. Just microwave them a pot pie. Share your cheese, or cottage cheese. Cook them an omelet. Give them chicken, hamburger, fish, steak, and vegetables. Potatoes in any form. Peanut butter sandwiches, or on crackers. Leftovers from eating out. Hash and eggs. Canned meats of any kind. Baby food for cats and small dogs. Once a week cook a large meatloaf with all kinds of stuff in it and give them a slice every day. Raw hamburger every once in a while, is fine. Cooked corn in cream or butter.

Consider (baking at 225°F overnight) liver, kidneys, necks, gizzards, hearts, or any animal parts normally not consumed by humans, and give all your pets a portion every day.

Be wary of cheap commercial foods. The price pretty much dictates the quality; you get what you pay for. Cut-rate pet foods are like "prisoner of war" food, designed to provide enough calories to stay alive, not maintain the individual to a ripe old age. Much of it is literally undigestible, resulting in excess stool formation and gas. Much of it is one step away from being used for fertilizer. You get what you pay for.

Be aware that it is actually cheaper to cook for your pets than buying the high-end foods offered in boutique pet shops, or supermarket pet stores.

Variety and diversity, just like your eating habits, is essential.

Alternate manufacturers. There is no way to tell what they change. Just because you have had good results in the past doesn't mean you will have the same results in the future.

Do not listen to, or bother looking at, any pet food ads. Pet food marketing is worse than a joke. It can actually be detrimental.

Read the labels and look up the ingredients as listed in Appendix 1, the AAFCO definitions of pet food ingredients.

Don't waste your time and money with supplements. Just feed fresh whole foods instead.

The larger brands of pet foods do a better job of consistently formulating food than off-brands.

Don't feed your cat kibble. Period. (Canned *Fancy Feast* is not bad.)

And finally, finally:

For heaven's sake, clean their teeth. The blood going through their mouths is picking up filth and puss and distributing it all over the body. They swallow that nasty stuff all day long.

Short of cooking for your pet, keeping their mouth clean is the nicest thing you can do for them. It is just plain cruel letting pets endure literally life-threatening dental disease. The suffering must be awful. And don't worry about them losing some teeth during the procedure. If the teeth are bad enough to come out, the pet isn't using them anyway. Ever have a toothache? I swear, I don't know how some of these little guys soldier on.

And take them to the groomer once in a while.

CHAPTER 12
HUMAN-ONLY SECTION

Prized foodie info—
so…
You can be a nutritional snob
and…
Impress your dinner guests.

1. Dark chocolate (over 70% cocoa) slows cancer cell growth by interrupting its blood supply (contains antioxidants, proanthocyanins, and polyphenols). Contains more of these than a glass of red wine.

Its capacity to raise blood sugar is less than white bread.

One-fifth of a bar a day. Zest with grated ginger, orange, or tangerine peel.

Melt over fruit.

Milk cancels the benefits—so no ice cream. No milk chocolate.

Serve with red wine and green tea.

2. Red wine has resveratrol (a really nice polyphenol) that comes from grape skin and seeds and transfers into wine due to fermentation.

Pinot noir from Burgundy, France, is superbly high in resveratrol.

White wine, grape juice, and raisins don't cut it (alcohol prevents oxidation and reduction of resveratrol).

Resveratrol works with your anti-aging genes, and blocks NF-kappa B, which causes cancer.

3. Green tea has high polyphenols, which retards vessels that supply cancers. It also makes cancer cells commit suicide. It also helps the liver get rid of toxins, which is good because that is one of the main jobs of the liver—gathering toxins. Stiffness can be toxin build up in the muscles because the liver isn't doing its job well.

Black tea is not as good because it is fermented, which destroys polyphenols. (I know, I said red wine has more polyphenols because of fermentation—told you this could get technical. Answer: One is fermented in carbon dioxide, and other one is fermented in oxygen. Guess which.)

Steep for 8 minutes, drink within one hour, doesn't store well, decaf is fine.

4. Agave nectar is a sweetener from cactus sap. (Cactus sap is used to make tequila.) It is three times sweeter than sugar but causes five times less of a blood sugar spike than honey. Great in drinks, on fruit, cereal, and so on.

5. Mushrooms contain polysaccharides and lentinan. These stimulate health of the immune system. Find an oriental grocery and buy them all and cook them any way and serve with anything.

6. Tomatoes and tomato sauce release lycopene when cooked and this helps slow down prostate cancer. Olive oil aids assimilation. Eat two or three times a week.

7. Ginger root is better than vitamin E in its anti-inflammatory and antioxidant effect. It starves cancer cells by preventing blood supply to tumors. It can help with nausea when sliced and steeped in boiling water and drunk hot or cold.

Grate into vegetable mix during cooking or marinate with fruit in citrus juice and agave nectar.

8. Brussels sprouts, bok choy, Chinese cabbage, broccoli, cauliflower contain sulforaphane and indole-3-carbinol that fight cancer and detoxify cancer-causing substances. They cause cancer cells to commit suicide.

Don't boil cabbage or broccoli, as it destroys the sulforaphane. Bake, steam, fry with olive oil.

9. Garlic, onions, leeks, shallots, and chives go back thousands of years. Garlic was used as a wound dressing during war, clear up through WWII. Nicknamed Russian penicillin. Louis Pasteur documented its antibacterial properties.

All these help regulate blood sugar levels, so they reduce insulin peaks.

Nitrosamines and N-nitroso compounds are created when meat is over grilled and are carcinogenic. These substances reduce those effects when cooked with meat.

Garlic works best when crushed and more assimilated when dissolved in oil.

They can be eaten raw. Many cultures suck on garlic cloves. Try growing some. The cloves grow under the ground like potatoes. Fresh, they are amazing. You can see why people eat them raw and with mayonnaise and bread.

10. Soy should not be powdered, then cooked. It should be soaked whole before processing or cooking. It blocks sex hormones from stimulating cancers with isoflavones. Asian women have fewer breast cancers or have less aggressive forms if they have eaten soy their whole life.

Tofu takes on the taste of other ingredients so it is fun to cook with.

11. Turmeric in curry is a powerful anti-inflammatory. More can be added to curry as sometimes curry doesn't have plenty. It also is used for reducing cholesterol.

Keep some prepared for use on vegetables, in soups, and salad dressings: tablespoon of turmeric, two tablespoons of olive oil, teaspoon of cracked black pepper. Add a little agave nectar to neutralize acrimony.

12. Seaweed. Edibles are nori, kombu, wakame, arame, and dulse. They can be cooked with or added to soup, salad, beans, lentils, garlic, peas, soybeans, peanuts, carob, potatoes, noodles, eggs, and fish. Nori seaweed contains lots of omega-3 essential fatty acids.

Seaweed stimulates immune cells, has carotenoids, and is even more effective in combating prostate cancer than cooked tomatoes.

13. Omega-3 essential fatty acid from fatty fish or high-quality fish oil supplements reduces inflammation and reduces cancer cell growth. Because large fish are high on the food chain and accumulate mercury, PCBs, and dioxin which pollute the ocean floor, small fish are the best sources. These include anchovies, mackerel, and sardines preserved in olive oil. If preserved in other oils the omega-6s outweigh the fish omega-3s.

Salmon is considered still considered a safe source of omega-3s.

14. Flaxseed is rich in omega-3s, and also has anti-estrogen lignans that block prostate cancer growth.

Flax seed can be ground in a coffee bean grinder and added to salad, cereal, yogurt, sour cream, tofu, vegetables, anything. It has a nutty flavor. Flax seed oil should be stored in the refrigerator in the dark.

15. Probiotics are just bacteria that are so called "friendly." Lactobacillus acidophilus is found in active culture yogurt, non-pasteurized buttermilk, sauerkraut, and Korean kimchi. Anything fermented. It can be taken in capsule form. These bacteria crowd out unfriendly bacteria that cause intestinal enteritis and gas formation. They work with **prebiotics,** which is just food they like to eat, pretty much any vegetable available. Sugar beet pulp is a good prebiotic. It has less sugar in it than a carrot.

V-8 is good for you. Make an aspic molded salad using unflavored gelatin and V-8. Add onions, sliced olives, celery, and hardboiled eggs. Serve with a dollop of canola/olive oil mayonnaise.

Nutritional snob dinner menu:

Have your guests watch all preparation and casually explain the benefits of each ingredient…anti-breast and prostate cancer, tumor suicide, isoflavones, really nice polyphenols, omega-3s, Russian penicillin (vodka), probiotic and anti-gas, and so on. Crib notes are allowed. It's best to pull ingredients from regular storage areas, with consternation and frowns indicating deep thought and creativity…as if you are making these fabrications as you go, with careless carefree abandon and an adoration of your ingredients' very existence. You want to be thought of as fluent in "kitchen."

This dinner party will deliver an explosion of flavors, and everything is contributing to robust health. It is educational as well. You will be thought of as a famous man, or woman, or couple, of the world.

1. Serve Tequila Sunrise cocktails: in a big tall glass with ice: mix tequila (stay away from top shelf—you want it rough and raw) and fresh squeezed orange juice, then pour crème de cassis gently down one side of the glass, and grenadine syrup down the other side. Crème de cassis is plum-purple, grenadine is red—when swirling in the orange juice it looks like a sunrise. Use a straw so people can make their own sunrises.

Offer thinly sliced carrots and celery, blanched asparagus and green beans, radish, small chunks of high-gluten baguette, and dipping oil made from olive oil, pepper, salt, ground flax seed, and fresh-grated parmesan cheese.

2. Open the wine, red, always two bottles open at all times—indicates abundance—fosters inebriation, which is compulsory for superior dinner parties. The wine should be rather light but not sweet. Drinkable. Just a beverage—not memorable. Fresh as opposed to moldy and woody and smoky. No sulfur. Quenching and taste clearing. This year's French Pinot usually makes a nice with-food wine—not overpowering—guests tend to swill it, making for a delightful party. (You may even want to decant it into a pitcher to make it even less spectacular.)

3. Make a salad with any mixed, washed and dried, chilled greens that look good. Add seaweed, green onions or lentils, thinly sliced hardboiled brown range-free eggs with a few drops of balsamic vinegar on the yolk, sliced mixed olives. Toss gently with a Caesar dressing (has anchovies in it) with some of your *turmeric-olive oil-course ground black* pepper added. Add small tofu cubes that have been rolled in olive oil, rosemary, and thyme, slices of tangerine, and a crumbly grass-fed feta cheese.

   Mortar and pestle Muntok white peppercorns, Tellicherry black peppercorns, Jamaican Allspice, pink peppercorns, and green peppercorns, and sprinkle on top with chopped almonds and walnuts.

   Don't make the salad too big.

4. Serve one small scoop of an ice or citrus sherbet in a champagne glass.

5. Broil, bake, steam, or grill individual serving-sized salmon filets with salt, crushed garlic, grass-fed cow's butter, fresh squeezed lemon, and chives. (Baking fish for 8-10 minutes at 500 degrees is always a success story, only don't use butter—peanut oil or olive oil have higher flashpoints.)

   Sauté sliced mixed mushrooms of your choice in lightly salted butter and champagne to top the salmon with when serving.

6. Accompany the salmon with sliced cherry and Italian tomatoes, halved Brussels sprouts, broccoli collarets, and small pieces of cauliflower baked in curried chicken stock. Add extra turmeric. Garnish with fresh chopped parsley.

7. Provide iced green tea with mint leaves (make ice with premium bottled spring water and boast about it). Use Agave nectar—no table sugar. Have a chilled bottled premium spring water on the table with a separate glass—no ice cubes.

8. For dessert pour melted (preferably use a double boiler) dark chocolate over sliced pear (marinated in tangerine juice, ginger, and agave nectar), black and red raspberries, and strawberries. Zest with tangerine peel. Serve with cold champagne and pressed decaf coffee in warmed cups with cinnamon and agave nectar. (No cream allowed—you can explain.)

9. Bring out the Grappa liqueur. Spent grapes, leaves, vines are fermented and distilled to make an excellent complex brandy. Or just sip tiny portions of any distilled product.

APPENDIX 1

AAFCO INGREDIENT DEFINITIONS

The following is the AAFCO (Association of American Feed Control Officials) definitions of ingredients used in pet food manufacture.

ALFALFA MEAL - the aerial (above ground) portion of the alfalfa plant, reasonably fee from other crop plants, weeds, and mold, which has been sun cured and finely ground.

ANIMAL DIGEST - material which results from chemical and/or enzymatic hydrolysis of clean and un-decomposed animal tissue. The animal tissues use shall be exclusive of hair, horns, teeth, hooves and feathers, except in such trace amounts as might occur unavoidably in good factory practice and shall be suitable for animal feed.

ANIMAL FAT - is obtained from the tissues of mammals and/or poultry in the commercial processes of rendering or extracting. It consists predominantly of glyceride esters of fatty acids and contains no additions of free fatty acids. If an antioxidant is used, the common name or manes must be indicated, followed by the words "used as a preservative."

BARLEY - consists of at least 80% sound barley and must not contain more than 3% heat-damaged kernels, 6% foreign material, 20% other grains or 10% wild oats.

BARLEY FLOUR - soft, finely ground and bolted (sifted to remove heavier, larger pieces of bran while leaving most of the germ) obtained from the milling of barley. It consists essentially of the starch and gluten of the endosperm.

BEEF (meat) - is the clean flesh derived from slaughtered cattle, and is limited to that part of the striate muscle which is skeletal or that which is found in the tongue, in the diaphragm, in the heart, or in the esophagus; with or without the accompanying and overlying fat and the portions of the skin, sinew, nerve and blood vessels which normally accompany the flesh.

BEET PULP ("beet pulp, dried molasses" and "beet pulp, dried, plain") - the dried residue from sugar beets.

BREWER'S RICE - the dried extracted residue of rice resulting from the manufacture of wort (liquid portion of malted grain) or beer and may contain pulverized dried spent hops in an amount not to exceed 3%.

BROWN RICE - unpolished rice after the kernels have been removed. Not a complete AAFCO definition.

CARROTS - presumably carrots. No AAFCO definition.

CHICKEN - the clean combination of flesh and skin with or without accompanying bone, derived from the parts or whole carcasses of chicken or a combination thereof, exclusive of feathers, heads, feet and entrails.

CHICKEN BYPRODUCT MEAL - consists of the ground, rendered, clean parts of the carcass of slaughtered chicken, such as necks, feet, undeveloped eggs and intestines, exclusive of feathers, except in such amounts as might occur unavoidable in good processing practice.

CHICKEN LIVER MEAL - chicken livers which have been ground otherwise reduced in particle size.

CHICKEN MEAL - chicken which has been ground or otherwise reduced in particle size.

CORN - unspecified corn product. Not a complete AAFCO definition.

CORN BRAN - the outer coating of the corn kernel, with little or none of the starchy part of the germ.

CORN GERM MEAL (DRY MILLED) - ground corn germ which consists of corn germ with other parts of the corn kernel from which part of the oil has been removed and is the product obtained in the dry milling process of manufacture of cornmeal, corn grits, hominy feed, and other corn products.

CORN GLUTEN - that part of the commercial shelled corn that remains after the extraction of the larger portion of the starch, gluten, and term by the processes employed in the wet milling manufacture of corn starch or syrup.

CORN GLUTEN MEAL - the dried residue from corn after the removal of the larger part of the starch and germ, and the separation of the bran by the process employed in the wet milling manufacture of corn starch or syrup, or by enzymatic treatment of the endosperm.

CORN SYRUP - concentrated juice derived from corn.

CRACKED PEARL BARLEY - cracked pearl barley resulting from the manufacture of pearl barley from clean barley.

DEHYDRATED EGGS - dried whole poultry eggs freed of moisture by thermal means.

DIGEST OF BEEF - material from beef which results from chemical and/or enzymatic hydrolysis of clean and un-decomposed tissue. The tissues used shall be exclusive of hair, horns, teeth and hooves, except in such trace amounts as might occur unavoidable in good factory practice.

DIGEST OF BEEF BYPRODUCTS - material from beef which results from chemical and/or enzymatic hydrolysis of clean and un-decomposed tissue but is not limited to, lungs, spleen, kidneys, brain, livers, bone, blood, partially defatted low temperature fatty tissue, and stomachs and intestines freed of their contents. It does not include hair, horns, teeth and hoofs.

DIGEST OF POULTRY BYPRODUCTS - material which results from chemical and/or enzymatic hydrolysis of clean and un-decomposed tissue from non-rendered clean parts of carcasses of slaughtered poultry such as heads, feet, viscera, free from fecal content and foreign matter except in such trace amounts as might occur unavoidably in good factory practice.

DRIED ANIMAL DIGEST - dried material resulting from chemical and/or enzymatic hydrolysis of clean and un-decomposed animal tissue. The animal tissue used shall be exclusive of hair, horns, teeth, hooves, and feathers, except in such trace amounts as might occur unavoidable in good factory practice and shall be suitable for animal feed. If it bears a name descriptive of its kind or flavor(s), it must correspond thereto.

DRIED KELP - dried seaweed of the families Laminaricae and Fucaeae. If the product is prepared by artificial drying it may be called "dehydrated kelp."

DRIED MILK PROTEIN - obtained by drying the coagulated protein residue resulting from the controlled co-precipitation of casein, lactalbumin and minor mild proteins from defatted milk.

DRIED REDUCED LACTOSE WHEY - no AAFCO definition available.

DRIED WHEY - the product obtained by removing water from the whey. It contains not less than 11 percent protein nor less than 61 percent lactose.

FEEDING OATMEAL - obtained in the manufacture of rolled oat groats or tolled oats and consists of broken oat groats, oat groat chips, and floury portions of the oat groats, with only such quantity of finely ground oat hulls as is unavoidable in the usual process of commercial milling. It must not contain more than 4% crude fiber.

FISH MEAL - the clean, dried, ground tissue of un-decomposed whole fish or fish cuttings, either or both, with or without the extraction of part of the oil.

GROUND CORN (ground ear corn) - the entire ear of corn ground, without husks, with no greater portion of cob than occurs in the ear corn in its natural state.

GROUND DE-HULLED OATS - presumably ground cleaned oats with hulls removed (ground oat groats). Not an AAFCO definition.

GROUND WHEAT - presumably a coarser grind of wheat flour. Not an AAFCO definition.

GROUND WHOLD BROWN RICE (GROUND BROWN RICE) - the entire product obtained by grinding the rice kernels after the hulls have been removed.

GROUND WHOLE WHEAT - ground whole kernel, presumably equivalent to AAFCO's Wheat Mill Run, Wheat Middlings, Wheat Shorts, or Wheat Red Dog, whose principal differences are in the percentage of crude fiber.

GROUND YELLOW CORN - same as ground corn, except that the corn used is yellow in color.

KIBBLED CORN - obtained by cooking cracked corn under steam pressure and extruding from an expeller or other mechanical pressure device.

LAMB BONE MEAL - (steamed) dried and ground product sterilized by cooking un-decomposed bones with steam under pressure. Grease, gelatin, and meat fiber may or may not be removed.

LAMB DIGEST - material resulting from chemical and/or enzymatic hydrolysis of clean and un-decomposed lamb. The tissue used shall be exclusive of hair, horns, teeth and hooves, except in such trace amounts as might occur unavoidably in good factory practice and shall be suitable for animal feed.

LAMB FAT - obtained from the tissues of lamb in the commercial processes of rendering or extracting. It consists predominantly of glyceride esters of fatty acids and contains no additions of free fatty acids. If an antioxidant is used, the common name or manes must be indicated, followed by the words "used as a preservative."

LAMB MEAL - the rendered product from lamb tissues, exclusive of blood, hair, hoof, horn, hide trimmings, manure, and stomach and rumen contents except in such amounts as may occur unavoidably in good processing practices.

LINSEED MEAL - the product obtained by grinding the cake or chip which remain after removal of most of the oil from flaxseed by a mechanical extraction process. It must contain no more than 10% fiber. The words "mechanical extracted" are not required when listing as an ingredient in the manufactured food.

LIVER - the hepatic gland (of whatever species is listed).

MEAT AND BONE MEAL - the rendered product from mammal tissues including bone, exclusive of blood, hair, hoof, horn, hide trimmings, manure, stomach and rumen contents, except in such amounts as may occur unavoidably in good processing practices.

MEAT BYPRODUCTS - the non-rendered, clean parts, other than meat, derived from slaughtered mammals. It includes, but is not limited to, lungs, spleen, kidneys, brain, livers, blood, bone, partially defatted low-temperature fatty tissue and stomachs and intestines freed of their contents. It does not include hair, horns, teeth and hooves.

MEAT MEAL - the rendered product from mammal tissues, exclusive of blood, hair, hoof, horn, hide trimmings, manure, stomach and rumen contents except in such amounts as may occur unavoidably in good processing practices.

PEAS - peas.

POTATOES - potatoes.

POULTRY BYPRODUCT MEAL - consists of the ground, rendered, clean parts of the carcass of slaughtered poultry, such as necks, feet, undeveloped eggs, intestines, exclusive of feathers, except in such amounts as might occur unavoidable in good processing practices.

POULTRY DIGEST - material which results from chemical and/or enzymatic hydrolysis of clean and un-decomposed poultry tissue.

POULTRY FAT (FEED GRADE) - primarily obtained from the tissue of poultry in the commercial process of rendering or extracting. It shall contain only the fatty matter natural to the product produced under good manufacturing practices and shall contain no added free fatty acids or other materials obtained from fat. It must contain not less than 90 percent total fatty acids and not more than 3 percent of un-saponifiagles and impurities. It shall have a minimum titer of 33 degrees Celsius. If an antioxidant is used, the common name or names must be indicated, followed by the word "preservative(s)."

POWDERED CELLULOSE - purified, mechanically disintegrated cellulose prepared by processing alpha cellulose obtained as pulp from fibrous plant materials.

RICE BRAN- the pericarp or bran layer and germ of the rice, with only such quantity of hull fragments, chipped, broken, or brewer's rice, and calcium carbonate as is unavoidable in the regular milling of edible rice.

RICE FLOUR

SOY FLOUR

SOYBEAN HULLS - consist primarily of the outer covering of the soybean.

SOYBEAN MEAL (DE-HULLED, SOLVENT EXTRACTED) - obtained by grinding the flakes remaining after removal of most of the oil from de-hulled soybeans by a solvent extraction process.

SOYBEAN MEAL (MECHANICAL EXTRACTED) - obtained by grinding the cake or chips which remain after removal of most of the oil from the soybeans by a mechanical extraction process.

SOYBEAN MILL RUN - composed of soybean hulls and such bean meats that adhere to the hulls which results from normal milling operations in the production of de-hulled soybean meal.

TALLOW - animal fats with titer above 40 degrees Celsius.

TURKEY - unspecified turkey. Not a complete AAFCO description.

TURKEY MEAL - the ground clean combination of flesh and skin with or without accompanying bone, derived from the parts or whole carcasses of turkey of a combination thereof, exclusive of feathers, heads, feet, and entrails.

WHEAT BRAN - the coarse outer covering of the wheat kernel as separated from cleaned and scoured wheat in the usual process of commercial milling.

WHEAT FLOUR - wheat flour together with fine particles of wheat bran, wheat germ and the offal from the "tail of the mill." This product must be obtained in the usual process of commercial milling and must not contain more than 1.5 percent crude fiber.

WHEAT GERM MEAL - consists chiefly of wheat germ together with some bran and middlings or short. It must contain not less than 25 percent crude protein and 7 percent crude fat.

WHEAT MILL RUN - coarse wheat bran, fine particles of wheat bran, wheat shorts, wheat germ, wheat flour and the offal from the "tail of the mill." This product must be obtained in the usual process of commercial milling and must contain no more than 9.5 percent crude fiber.

WHEY - the product obtained as a fluid by separating the coagulum from milk, cream or skimmed milk and from which portion of the milk fat may have been removed.

APPENDIX 2

14 KINDS OF VITAMINS

Vitamin A: In liver, meat, fish, eggs, and dairy products. Important for vision, pulmonary function, and skin.

Vitamin D: In tuna, sardines, egg yolk, dairy products. Regulates calcium absorption, and prevents loss.

Vitamin E: Liver, meat, eggs, dairy, grains. Antioxidant, immune system, neurological, vision, skin.

Vitamin K: Meat, vegetables. Cofactor in many enzymes, blood coagulation, anemia, hemorrhage.

B1 - thiamine: Meat, bran, wheat, yeast. Involved in many biochemical reactions including generating energy in cells, and maintaining the integrity of the nervous system.

B2 - riboflavin: Yeast, liver, cheese, eggs, dairy. Helps turn fat into energy.

B5 - pantothenic acid: Meat, eggs, dairy. Part of coenzyme A which is involved in every metabolic reaction and creation of energy in cells.

B6 - pyridoxine: Yeast, wheat, meat, dairy. In many reactions as a coenzyme specifically amino acid metabolism.

B12 - cobalamin: Manufactured by friendly bacteria in the intestine. Essential for the production of red blood cells.

Niacin: In most foods. Skin health and breaking down sugars and fats into energy.

B8 - biotin: In most foods. Participates in the same functions as niacin.

B9 - folic acid: Liver, vegetables, spinach, yeast, cheese. Important for pregnancy; helps synthesize DNA. Fetus needs a great deal causing the mother to develop a deficiency.

Choline & inositol: Meat, eggs, liver, heart, nuts. Cell membrane and nerve conduction and protects skin from dehydration.

Vitamin C: All vegetables and fruits and berries. Made by dogs and cats, but not humans. Helps in illness, aging, cell stress, and joint issues.

APPENDIX 3

USEFUL SOURCES

AAFCO (Association of American Feed Control Officials), www. aafco.org

American Academy of Veterinary Nutrition, www.aavm.org

American College of Veterinary Nutrition, www.acvn.org

American Society of Clinical Nutrition, www.nutrition.org

Consumerlab.com tests dietary supplements for purity, potency, bioavailability, etc., www.comsumerlab.com

FDA Center for Food Safety and Applied Nutrition-regulatory and safety issues, adverse event reporting, meetings, industry information, http://vm.cfsan.fda.gov/dms/supplmnt.html

FDA Center for Veterinary Medicine, www.fda.gov/cvm

FDA Recall List, www.fda.gov/opacom/7alerts.HTML

Mayo Clinic Drugs and Supplements Information, www. mayoclinic. com/health/drug-information/DrugHerbIndex

NIH National Center for Complementary and Alternative Medicine, http://nccam.nih.gov

NIH Office of Dietary Supplements (fact sheets, safety notices, database, http://dietary-supplements.info.nih.gov

Pet Food Institute, www.petfoodinstiture, www.petfoodreport.org.

USDA Food and Nutrition Information Center (general supplement and nutrition information, links to a variety of dietary supplement websites), www.nal.usda.gov/fnic/etext/000015.html

United State Pharmacopeia Dietary Supplement Verification Program (voluntary program) www.usp-dsvp.org.

Information on producers concerned with proper nutrition for food producing animals: www.americangrassfed.com and www.eatwild.com. David Servan-Schreiber, MD, Ph.D., *Anti-Cancer, A New Way of Life,* Viking Press, 2008. This book describes natural diets and methods of anti-cancer healthcare that complement conventional medical care. Standard Process Inc., P.O. Box 904, Palmyra, WI 53156, www.standardprocess. com.www.mercoplahealthypets.com

Beth Taylor & Karen Shaw Becker, DVM, *Real Food for Healthy Dogs & Cats,* Natural Pet Productions, 2011, www. naturalpetproductions.com. Marion Nestle Ph.D. & Malden C. Nesheim Ph.D. *Feed Your Pet Right,* Free Press, 2010, www. foodpolitics.com.

Fox, Hodgkins, Smart, *Not Fit for a Dog,* Quill Driver Books, 2009. Richard Pitcairn, DVM, Ph.D., *Dr. Pitcairn's Complete Guide to Natural Health for Dogs & Cats.* Holtzbrinck Publishers, 2005.

Ann N. Martin, *Food Pets Die For,* NewSage Press, 2008.

Hand, Thatcher, Remillard, Roudebush, *Small Animal Clinical Nutrition,* Walsworth Publishing, 2000.

Mark Poveromo, *To Your Dog's Health,* Poor Man's Press, 2010.

Ihor John Basko DVM, *Fresh Food & Ancient Wisdom, Preparing Healthy & Balanced Meals for Your Pets.* Makana Kai Publishing, www.DrBasko.com.

Alexandra Horowitz, *Inside of a Dog,* Scribner, 2009.

Goodman, Gilman, *The Pharmacological Basis of Therapeutics,* Macmillan, 1970.

Lewis, Morris, Hand, *Small Animal Clinical Nutrition,* Mark Morris Associates, 1987.

ABOUT THE AUTHOR

As a veterinarian for over 40 years, Dr. Jarvis Williams has treated everything from parakeets to pachyderms. He has traveled the world observing how different cultures feed their dogs and cats. He has devoted his life to thousands of animals in his care, helping them to live long, healthy, and happy lives.

I appreciate you reading my book! Can you leave a comment and a star rating on Amazon? Help me get THE TRUTH out there!

My website is loaded with pet related blogs, photos, recipes, and links to other authors and websites, for dogs and cats. Take a photo trip on how to use a turkey roaster to make a lot of pet food fast and cheap! Go to my website: www.jarviswrites.page

Sign up with your email and receive offers, updates, freebees, and sneak peeks of 8 soon to be published books. Join my launch team (on my website) and get all my books free before anyone else. (We promise not to abuse your time and will only ding you every other week or so... unless we have a warning, recall, new disease, etc.)

Thanks again every one of you! Dr. W.

9 781737 916710